PUBLICATIONS OF THE DEPARTMENT OF ROMANCE LANGUAGES
UNIVERSITY OF NORTH CAROLINA

General Editor: ALDO SCAGLIONE

Editorial Board: JUAN BAUTISTA AVALLE-ARCE, PABLO GIL CASADO, FRED M. CLARK, GEORGE BERNARD DANIEL, JANET W. DÍAZ, ALVA V. EBERSOLE, AUGUSTIN MAISSEN, EDWARD D. MONTGOMERY, FREDERICK W. VOGLER

NORTH CAROLINA STUDIES IN THE ROMANCE LANGUAGES AND LITERATURES

ESSAYS; TEXTS, TEXTUAL STUDIES AND TRANSLATIONS; SYMPOSIA

Founder: URBAN TIGNER HOLMES

Editor: JUAN BAUTISTA AVALLE-ARCE
Associate Editor: FREDERICK W. VOGLER

Other publications of the Department: *Estudios de Hispanófila, Hispanófila, Romance Notes, Studia Raeto-Romanica*

Distributed by:

INTERNATIONAL SCHOLARLY BOOK SERVICE, INC.
P. O. BOX 4347
Portland, Oregon   97208
U. S. A.

NORTH CAROLINA STUDIES IN THE
ROMANCE LANGUAGES AND LITERATURES

Essays 6

GIDE'S ART OF THE FUGUE
A THEMATIC STUDY OF "LES FAUX-MONNAYEURS"

GIDE'S ART OF THE FUGUE

A THEMATIC STUDY OF "LES FAUX-MONNAYEURS"

BY

KARIN NORDENHAUG CIHOLAS

CHAPEL HILL

NORTH CAROLINA STUDIES IN THE
ROMANCE LANGUAGES AND LITERATURES
U.N.C. DEPARTMENT OF ROMANCE LANGUAGES

1974

Library of Congress Cataloging in Publication Data

Ciholas, Karin Nordenhaug.
　Gide's art of the fugue.

　(North Carolina studies in the Romance languages and literatures: Essay; 6).
　Bibliography: p. 124.
　1. Gide, André Paul Guillaume, 1869-1951. Les faux-monnayeurs. I. Title. II. Series: North Carolina studies in the Romance languages and literatures: Essays; 6.

PQ2613.I2F333   843'.9'12   74-26588

ISBN: 978-0-8078-9153-7

DEPÓSITO LEGAL: V. 4.044 - 1974
ARTES GRÁFICAS SOLER, S. A. - JÁVEA, 28 - VALENCIA (8) - 1974

To the memory of my father
JOSEF NORDENHAUG

ACKNOWLEDGMENTS

I am indebted to Professors George B. Daniel and Siegfried E. Mews for their valuable suggestions and encouragement. To Professor Eugene H. Falk who has been both mentor and friend no words can adequately express my gratitude. His scholarship and respect for the work of art will be a lifelong inspiration. Permission to use quotations from Gide's Les Faux-Monnayeurs *was obtained from Éditions Gallimard.*

K. N. C.

Centre College
Danville, Kentucky

CONTENTS

Pages

INTRODUCTION ... 13

CHAPTER I: THE FLASHLIGHT AND THE SCISSORS: STRUCTURAL PROBLEMS IN 'LES FAUX-MONNAYEURS' ... 17

CHAPTER II: EDOUARD VERSUS GIDE: THE DILEMMA OF THE CRITIC ... 28

CHAPTER III: THE INTEGRITY OF THE WORK OF ART: THEMATIC ANALYSIS AS A CRITICAL METHOD ... 37

CHAPTER IV: IDENTITY AND DESTINY: CENTRAL THEMES OF THE STORY ... 50

CHAPTER V: THE SPHINX OF SELF-DELUSION: THEMES OF THE PLOT ... 62

CHAPTER VI: LUX ET VERITAS: GENERIC COHERENCE OF THEMES ... 87
    The Problem of Reality ... 87
    Conscious and Unconscious Blindness ... 93
    Apollo and Daphne ... 99
    The Counterfeit Coin ... 104
    Cut-off Hands ... 109
    The Automaton ... 111
    The Wilting Flower ... 114
    Salt and Light ... 116

CONCLUSION ... 122

BIBLIOGRAPHY ... 124

INTRODUCTION

Few authors have left behind as extensive an account of their life, work, and thought as André Gide whose concern with the literary world often transcended literature to encompass an entire philosophy of life. His famous precept, "assumer le plus possible d'humanité", places his aspirations beyond the literary realm of activity. His constant endeavor to reveal himself as truthfully and as objectively as possible has given posterity a rich documentation on his life as expressed in the numerous accounts of his travels, his autobiographical works, his prolific correspondence, and most notably the extensive scope of meticulously and faithfully kept Journals which cover more than half a century.

Thomas Mann called Gide the "contemporain capital" during a life conducted with "magnificent and conscientious candor".[1] Jean-Paul Sartre claimed he was one of the first to follow to its agonizing consequences his decision to live the anguish of the death of God.[2] Both of these eminent writers look at Gide as Gide the man before seeing Gide the writer, and quite possibly Gide enjoyed being viewed in this manner. Albert Guerard discusses him mainly as a moralist or "demoralizer". E. W. Knight makes his philosophical insights the essential factor of his writing and places him among the existentialists in outlook. Jean Delay undertakes the contemplation of Gide as the psychological case study of a man who was also a writer and uses incidents in the works to illustrate events of his life. Germaine Brée consciously

---

[1] Thomas Mann, "Gide's Unending Search for Harmony", Introduction to Albert J. Guerard, *André Gide*, (New York, 1963), p. vi.

[2] Jean-Paul Sartre, "Gide vivant", *Les Temps Modernes* (March 1951), p. 1540.

rejects any unliterary approach to his works, but is constantly brought back to Gide himself, seeks to grasp him, and finds him as elusive as Proteus. In general, it would seem that the study of Gide is more interesting than the study of Gide's work.

If literary criticism is to include the study of influences, of biographical factors and the unfathomable depths of the writer himself, we are dealing with a vast, inexhaustible field which encompasses most of the humanities. Such literary criticism is involved with sociological and psychological influences, with history as well as with philosophy and progressively leads us away from literature itself. Literature is considered as a result, a product of influences, not an entity within itself. Vinio Rossi claims that Gide's life cannot be dissociated from his work as an artist that "Gide lived his novels as though they were life." [3] The "as though" is reassuring and allows for the necessary distinction between the artist and his creation. We realize that each author as a unique individual creates a work which is also unique. Conrad said of the novelist: "...every novelist must begin by creating for himself a world, great or little, in which he can honestly believe. This world cannot be made otherwise than in his own image: it is fated to remain individual and a little mysterious." [4] There is no doubt that Gide put himself into his work, but what is true of Gide is also true of every other novelist. The difference so noticeable in Gide-scholarship is one of degree. The degree to which he put himself into his work is so great that his work is dangerously overshadowed by the man and his philosophy. The danger of the biographical approach resides in conclusions reached by such critics as J. B. Priestley who said: "Les Faux-Monnayeurs ...never comes to life as a novel. A born diarist and self-explainer, Gide is no creator." [5]

It is the objective of this study to dissociate the man and his work, to free the work from the overpowering presence of the man, and to study his magnum opus *Les Faux-Monnayeurs* in the unobstructed light of the work itself. If J. B. Priestley's

---

[3] Vinio Rossi, *André Gide: The Evolution of an Aesthetic* (New Brunswick, 1967), p. 4.

[4] Joseph Conrad, "Novel as World", *Theory of the Novel*, ed. Philip Stevick (New York, 1967), p. 29.

[5] J. B. Priestley, *Literature and Western Man* (New York, 1966), p. 414.

statement is true, there would be no "world" of the novel to study, and what I propose to do would be impossible. It is, however, my belief that Gide's novelistic world not only exists, but lives, and provides a rich source for study and analysis.

Gide complained in his *Journal* as early as 1921: "Les trois quarts des critiques, et presque tous ceux des journaux, se font leur opinion, non d'après mes livres eux-mêmes, mais d'après des conversations de café."[6] The emphasis he placed on the works themselves, in this case divorced from the popular opinion of them, justifies our concern for their integrity as artistic creations. But Gide was not offended merely because his own work was not receiving fair criticism, he was concerned for all works of art. In a lecture to a group of painters he defined the work of art explicitly: "The work of art is a work of the will. The work of art is a work of reason. For it must find in itself its sufficiency, its end, and its complete justification; forming a whole, it must be able to isolate itself and rest, as though out of space and time, in a satisfied and satisfying harmony."[7]

I have singled out *Les Faux-Monnayeurs* for a detailed analysis for three different reasons. First, this is the only work Gide himself called a novel and therefore represents a culminating moment in his achievements. Secondly, the fact that it relates the story of a novelist who expounds his theories on the novel has placed this work within the ranks of literary creations which will continuously whet the appetites of the critics. Thirdly, though the novel has never ceased to rouse interest it has never to my knowledge been analyzed in relationship to its thematic structure. Too often, it seems, the novel has stimulated interest merely for the theories Edouard expresses in it and for its "construction en abyme", even though the technique of a book within a book goes back as far as *Tristam Shandy* and *Heinrich von Ofterdingen*. Nor is it a new phenomenon in Gide's work. He used the technique of "construction en abyme" in his *Cahiers d'André Walter*, his *Traité de Narcisse*, and his *Tentative Amoreuse* and

---

[6] Gide, *Journal* I (Paris, 1960), Nov. 1921, p. 703; hereafter referred to as, *JAG*.
[7] Gide, "The Limits of Art", *Pretexts*, trans. Angelo P. Bertocci (New York, 1959), p. 46.

called it a "rétroaction du sujet sur lui-même".[8] The novelty of the novel and the consternation it has caused among critics lies rather in its structural complexity which, in my estimation, is counterbalanced by its thematic unity.

I shall discuss the structural problems of *Les Faux-Monnayeurs*, evaluate some of the critiques which have been formulated about it, and then proceed to submit the entire work to a thematic analysis using Professor Eugene H. Falk's method which will be explained and illustrated in Chapter three. My aim is to demonstrate that *Les Faux-Monnayeurs* is a unified composition based on an interrelationship of themes. By considering the themes in their linear and causal sequence and in their reciprocal relatedness based on their affinity of similarity or contrast I hope to prove that the novel's most outstanding compositional and artistic feature is its intrinsic coherence, its "satisfied and satisfying harmony".

---

[8] Gide, *JAG* I, p. 41.

Chapter I

THE FLASHLIGHT AND THE SCISSORS:
STRUCTURAL PROBLEMS IN 'LES FAUX-MONNAYEURS'

Every novel from the masterpiece of Proust's *A la recherche du temps perdu* to the tawdry pulp novel has some form of structural technique, whether it be a conscious system on the part of the author or not. Structure implies a process of composition. In the novel it deals with factors other than words, factors which according to their usage and disposition in the text affect both content and form. The structural elements of the novel are the angle, distance, or point of view from which the story is told, the types of narrators used, the time element of narration (which includes flashbacks and foreshadowing), the use of dialogue, interior monologue, and thought penetration, the interplay of dramatic and descriptive elements, the delineation of character, the concepts of story and plot, the occurrence of themes in their compositional relationships, the obvious necessity of a beginning, middle and end, the proportion of each structural element to other elements, and the more technical division into parts, books, and chapters.

Les Faux-Monnayeurs is divided into three parts of which the first and last take place in Paris and consist of exactly eighteen chapters each and are of almost equal length. The second part consists of seven chapters and takes place in Saas-Fée. The novel ascends to a plateau where the action is momentarily arrested and then plunges in ever increasing speed to its dénouement. Classical, like a tragedy, the structural balance is inherent in its skeletal framework.

The novel, however, is not a straight-forward, chronological account of a few basic characters and their interrelationships. The sequential enumeration of incidents in the story is possible, but rendered more difficult for the reader by the fact that Gide weaves the threads of the various incidents back and forth between past and present, between narrators and characters. Although Gide reveals one incident after another in the actual sequence of the book, he often interpolates large portions of narrative between incidents which happened at the very same time. It is the reader's task to relate the incidents in time even though they are separated in the book. The sequel of the story is also interrupted by Edouard's Journal, which relates incidents which happened before our story begins, and by the excerpt of the novel he is writing. In addition, six letters from various characters are inserted in the narrative.

We know from Gide's *Journal des Faux-Monnayeurs* that this very multiplicity of time sequences and incidents posed an unusual problem for him. He says:

> C'est à l'envers que se développe, assez bizarrement, mon roman. C'est-à-dire que je découvre sans cesse que ceci ou cela, qui se passait auparavant, devrait être dit. Les chapitres, ainsi, s'ajoutent, non point les uns après les autres, mais repoussant toujours plus loin celui que je pensais d'abord être le premier.[1]

In other words the novel evolved from the center outwards, whereas the central focal point is Edouard and the novel he is writing. Edouard's Journal not only serves the purpose of being the source for Edouard's future novel, but also gives us the background material for the understanding of incidents of the story as well as many aspects of the characters' motivations which reveal the plot. The very fact that Edouard provides us with many incidents of the story gives us the additional task of separating the purely factual material of his Journal from his own interpretation of it, which we fortunately learn to distrust very early, as one of Edouard's first comments is:

---

[1] "Journal des Faux-Monnayeurs", *Oeuvres Complètes*, XIII (Paris, 1932), p. 39. References to this edition are hereafter abbreviated, *OC*.

> Que cette question de la sincérité est irritante! *Sincérité!* Quand j'en parle, je ne songe qu'à sa sincérité à elle [Laura]. Si je me retourne vers moi, je cesse de comprendre ce que ce mot veut dire. Je ne suis jamais que ce que je crois que je suis — et cela varie sans cesse, de sorte que souvent, si je n'étais là pour les accointer, mon être du matin ne reconnaîtrait pas celui du soir.[2]

This inability to distinguish between reality and imagined reality will play a major rôle in the evaluation of Edouard's character in relationship to the entire novel, but for the thematic development of the story or plot derived from incidents related in his Journal we must constantly bear in mind that this is *Edouard's point of view*. The incidents not related in Edouard's Journal are told by anonymous narrators. One relates the events in the third person and past tense; the other appears when the action becomes more immediate and switches to the present tense and the first person in which Gide seems so much at home from his various *récits*.

The first-person-narrator who follows first one character and then another is apparently objective and *not* omniscient. He is limited by space and time; he cannot observe what Antoine is telling the maid in the kitchen, because he is more interested in observing Bernard at that particular moment. Although he would like to portray every single aspect of the story he is, by his spatial and temporal limitations, forced to selectivity. Paradoxically, however, the jump from one place to another takes no time and he remains invisible to those he observes. He never interferes in the story; he remains a narrator-witness and merely informs the reader. And yet he has a will of his own. When he suddenly decides to switch to other characters the reader is obligated to follow. Like the *Diable boiteux* he uncovers one roof and then another and penetrates into the characters' secrets. Perhaps this comparison with the picaresque is the most appropriate, for the intrusion of this narrator adds a flavor of impishness to the novel, an aura of Mephistophelean mischief, which reminds us of the remark Gide made in his *Journal des Faux-Monnayeurs*: "J'en voudrais un (le diable) qui circulerait

---

[2] *Les Faux-Monnayeurs* (Paris, 1925), p. 89. Gide's italics.

incognito à travers tout le livre et dont la réalité s'affirmerait d'autant plus qu'on croirait moins en lui." [3]

In long passages of the novel there is no first-person-narrator, merely an implied narrator [4] behind the scenes who listens in on the thoughts and interior monologues of various characters during their actions and describes their behavior. The very first sentence of the novel reveals what Bernard is saying to himself. It is interesting to note that this implied narrator as well as the first-person-narrator mentioned earlier describe actions, but seldom appearances or scenic detail. We learn in the very first chapter of *Les Faux-Monnayeurs* that Dhurmer is impatient with a novel that furnishes no descriptive information of color and form. This is doubly significant when we realize that the novel never gives us a physical description of Bernard or Edouard. We never learn what they actually look like, although they are so "real" in so many other ways that the reader probably carries a mental image of them after their very first appearance. It is Edouard, however, the man who professed to do away with realism in the novel, who offers us an abundance of descriptive detail. The implied narrator does give us visual descriptions of several characters. Significantly the characters we may visualize in the most detail from the information he offers are Vincent with his high forehead and his hair parted on one side, Lilian robed in purple pyjamas, and Passavant whose brown hair is slowly receding to reveal baldness. Descriptive information is often inserted into dialogue in order to let the reader visualize scene and character. Gide, however, has given us the most detail of physical description about characters of whom he shall say in his chapter 'L'auteur juge ses personnages': "De tels personnages sont taillés dans une étoffe sans épaisseur." [5] The surface is all that can be described since there is nothing underneath. It is in this chapter, where Gide stops to judge his characters, that we encounter a fourth angle of observa-

---

[3] "Journal des Faux-Monnayeurs", *OC XIII*, p. 21.

[4] The term "implied narrator" is preferable to Wayne C. Booth's "implied author" in "Distance and Point-of-View, An Essay in Classification", *Theory of the Novel*, op. cit., p. 92. Because of the authorial intrusion in the final chapter of Part II the term "author" is reserved for the one who calls himself that in the novel.

[5] *Les Faux-Monnayeurs*, p. 277.

tion. At a greater distance — Gide compares it to the traveler who has reached a mountaintop and looks down — the author analyzes his characters. The spell of uninterrupted illusion within the world of the novel itself is momentarily broken.

In discussing the narrative points of view of this novel we have gone from the center outward, from Edouard to the author, from subjectivity to objectivity. Edouard is in the middle encircled by the characters. Depending on the direction in which he is looking he sees either one character or another, one idea or another, but always in relationship to himself. The first-person-narrator is more objective; he is not an actual character in the traditional sense of the word, although speculation on his significance as the "diable incognito" is tempting. (Devils usually are.) The implied narrator has no subjective part in the novel whatsoever. The author who intrudes as author to discuss his characters is by that very intrusion one further step removed from the world of the story. And if we are to be wary of too readily indentifying Gide with this intrusive author, we must surmise that Gide himself is yet another distance removed from the story. The intrusive author may have a deeper insight than Edouard, but he is not omniscient either. He realizes some things are terribly wrong and he understands why. But he sees the future with foreboding not with certainty:

> Le voyageur, parvenu au haut de la colline, s'assied, et regarde avant de reprendre sa marche, à présent déclinante; il cherche à distinguer où le conduit enfin ce chemin sinueux qu'il a pris, qui lui semble se perdre dans l'ombre et, car le soir tombe, dans la nuit. Ainsi l'auteur imprévoyant s'arrête un instant, reprend souffle, et se demande avec inquiétude où va le mener son récit.[6]

In spite of Gide's comments that his characters were leading him whither he did not know, from his actual use of newspaper clippings we realize that Gide knew exactly where he was going, although at times he may not have known how to get there. Standing behind this intrusive author, therefore, is the gaunt figure of

---

[6] *Ibid.*, p. 274.

Gide, present on every page, yet not visible. We are faced with a combination of viewing angles.

In his discussion of *Point of View in Fiction* Friedman calls consistency of point of view a necessity of unity, but concludes "that when an author surrenders in fiction, he does so in order to conquer; he gives up certain privileges and imposes certain limits in order more effectively to render his story-illusion, which constitutes artistic truth in fiction." [7] Gide sacrificed the simplicity of consistency of point of view to the complexity of multiple viewing angles, because it revealed the artistic truth he was after.

Gide dedicated *Les Faux-Monnayeurs* to Roger Martin du Gard and it is to him that we owe the enlightening explanation of Gide's novelistic technique concerning point of view. Roger Martin du Gard is speaking of a conversation he had with Gide on the subject:

> Pour mieux se faire comprendre, il a pris une feuille blanche, y a tracé une ligne horizontale, toute droite. Puis, saisissant ma lampe de poche, il a promené lentement le point lumineux d'un bout à l'autre de la ligne: "Voilà votre *Barois*, voilà votre *Thibault*... Vous imaginez la biographie d'un personnage, ou l'historique d'une famille, et vous projetez là-dessus votre lumière, honnêtement, année par année ...Moi, voilà comment je veux composer mes *Faux-Monnayeurs*..." Il retourne la feuille, y dessine un grand demicercle, pose la lampe au milieu et, la faisant virer sur place, il promène le rayon tout au long de la courbe, en maintenant la lampe au point central: "Comprenez-vous, cher? Ce sont deux esthétiques. Vous, vous exposez les faits en historiographe, dans leur succession chronologique. C'est comme un panorama, qui se déroule devant le lecteur. Vous ne racontez jamais un événement passé à travers un événement présent. [8]

Since Gide explained it so graphically we can now see the structural technique behind his multiple points of view. Gide as extrinsic author is holding the flashlight on the half-circle of his characters. Within the half-circle surrounded by the same char-

---

[7] Norman Friedman, "Point of View in Fiction, the Development of a Critical Concept", *Theory of the Novel*, op. cit., p. 137.

[8] Roger Martin du Gard, *Oeuvres Complètes*, II (Paris, 1955), p. 1371.

acters stands Edouard who in turn is holding the light to the characters and occasionally on himself. Because Edouard is closer his view is less objective, and because the light from Gide's flashlight hits him also, the view the reader perceives of him is at once the one as seen through the eyes of Edouard and the one as seen through the eyes of Gide. To follow Gide's image to its conclusion the implied narrator and the first-person-narrator move up and down the circumference of the half-circle observing characters and situations within the light already projected upon them.

The characters are shown in an ever-changing light. Some are momentarily in the spotlight of attention and recede while others emerge from the shadows. The source of light is static, but the direction of projection is dynamic. As the moon changes its appearance in relationship to the light of the sun, so the characters change their shape in relationship to the spotlight. Depending on the angle at which the rays hit them the characters appear either "flat" or "round." [9] Thus as Vincent gradually disappears from the incidents of the novel his form loses depth and he becomes a caricature of evil which finally disappears into complete shadow where a ray of the spotlight hits him only indirectly one last time, since mention of him reaches the main spotlight of events only through a letter received by a marginal figure who conveys the message to a more central figure. In his *Journal des Faux-Monnayeurs* Gide redefines his aesthetic perspective:

> Je reprochais à Martin du Gard l'allure discursive de son récit; se promenant tout le long des années, sa lanterne de romancier éclaire toujours de face les événements qu'il considère, chacun de ceux-ci vient à son tour au premier plan; jamais leurs lignes ne se mêlent et, pas plus qu'il n'y a d'ombre, il n'y a de perspective. C'est déjà ce qui me gêne dans Tolstoi. Ils peignent des panoramas; l'art est de faire un tableau. Etudier *d'abord* le point d'où

---

[9] E. M. Forster's terms in *Aspects of the Novel* (New York, 1927), pp. 103-118. Forster's use of "flat" is more limited and refers to characters who do not evolve at all and who can be "expressed in one sentence". (p. 104).

> doit affluer la lumière; toutes les ombres en dépendent.
> Chaque figure repose et s'appuie sur son ombre.[10]

In the evaluation of story and plot as structural elements we encounter a problem of definition because of the laxity of popular usage. Plot has been frequently used to denote simply what happens in a novel, and many Plot Outlines available simply give a succinct enumeration of incidents in chronological order. The Aristotelean distinction between probability and necessity in the sequence of incidents is often disregarded. We cannot, however, overlook this distinction which enables us to define story and plot and which plays an important rôle in Falk's method of thematic analysis. I shall refer to his terms which he based on E. M. Forster's *Aspects of the Novel*, because Forster was, among modern critics, the closest to the Aristotelean distinction. Forster defines plot as a "narrative of events" with "the emphasis falling on causality."[11] In the plot the sequence of events is governed by *necessity*. The story Forster calls "a narrative of events arranged in their time sequence."[12] In the story the sequence of incidents is governed by *probability*.[13] In the plot the time sequence is still there, but the cause-effect relationship predominates. Plot and story are therefore intricately related to each other, but can be viewed separately as each satisfies a different need in the novelistic structure and conveys separate sets of themes. This will be further elaborated upon in the discussion of thematic analysis as a critical method, and a chapter each will be devoted to the themes of the story and the themes of the plot.

Henry James said that "the province of art is all life, all feeling, all observation, all vision."[14] Gide sought to make the province of *Les Faux-Monnayeurs* as inclusive as possible within the limitations imposed by the necessity of having a beginning, middle, and end. Inclusive of the problems of the young, the old, the middle-aged, inclusive of the conflicts between fiction and reality, inclusive of the very existence of the novel as a genre ...inclusive, but

---

[10] "Journal des Faux-Monnayeurs", *OC XIII*, p. 19.
[11] Forster, p. 130.
[12] Forster, p. 47.
[13] Eugene H. Falk, *Types of Thematic Structure* (Chicago, 1967), p. 5.
[14] Henry James, *The Future of the Novel* (New York, 1956), p. 20.

not conclusive. The technique of an open ending suggested in *L'Immoraliste*, experimented with in *Les Caves du Vatican*, is here carefully prepared in the course of the novel. Like life itself the subject of the novel goes on and on and never comes to rest.

Some people expect a symphony to end on the impressive chords of a Beethoven finale and cannot appreciate the abrupt silence which follows a Schönberg composition. In modern music as well as in the theatre it takes an education to know when to applaud. Because of the "sheer mental gymnastics" [15] which Carlos Lynes says it takes to appreciate Gide's novel there are those who grumble that the last page has left us dangling in mid air, when it has simply brought us back to the continuing reality of life itself. Critics have objected that this is precisely what a work of art should not do, that it, on the contrary, must infect us with "divine somnambulism" [16] where for the blissful moments of reading we might be oblivious to reality. Ortega y Gasset said that the novel must of an aesthetic necessity be impervious, "it must possess the power of forming a precinct, hermetically closed to all actual reality." [17] But what if the subject of the novel were to be the conflict between reality and fiction? After Conrad's "world" are we to be satisfied with Ortega's "precinct"?

Ortega y Gasset wrote his dire prediction of the decline of the novel at a moment when he earnestly believed that the novel, if not exhausted, was a least in its last phase because of the lack of new subject matter. [18] His essay was written in 1925 the very year Gide was placing the finishing but "non-conclusive" touches on *Les Faux-Monnayeurs*. A new world was opening up for the novel precisely because Gide did not want to restrict and confine his subject. An hermetically sealed "precinct" would have been the death blow to the modern novel, and in the light of the *Nouveau Roman* and its remarkable freedom of subject matter

---

[15] Carlos Lynes, "André Gide and the Problem of Form in the Novel", *Forms of Modern Fiction, Essays Collected in Honor of Joseph Warren Beach*, ed. William Van O'Connor (Minneapolis, 1948), p. 186.

[16] José Ortega y Gasset, "Notes on the Novel", *The Dehumanization of Art and Other Essays on Art, Culture, and Literature* (Princeton, 1968), p. 95.

[17] Ortega y Gasset, p. 94.

[18] *Ibid*, p. 60.

and technique *Les Faux-Monnayeurs* becomes merely one of the first works to have broken the bonds that restricted the novel.

Henry James has proved to be more prophetic than Ortega y Gasset, and at the turn of the century he envisioned both the perils and the infinite potential of the novel:

> ...the prose picture can never be at the end of its tether until it loses the sense of what it can do. It can do simply everything, and that is its strength and its life. Its plasticity, its elasticity are infinite; ...it moves in a luxurious independence of rules and restrictions. [19]

The infinite variety of subject matter of which the novel is capable was recognized by Gide's novelist-character Edouard who said:

> Mon roman n'a pas de sujet. Oui, je sais bien; ça a l'air stupide ce que je dis là. Mettons si vous préférez qu'il n'y aura pas *un* sujet... "Une tranche de vie", disait l'école naturaliste. Le grand défaut de cette école, c'est de couper sa tranche toujours dans le même sens; dans le sens du temps, en longueur. Pourquoi pas en largeur? ou en profondeur? Pour moi, je voudrais ne pas couper du tout. Comprenez-moi; je voudrais tout y faire entrer, dans ce roman. Pas de coup de ciseaux pour arrêter, ici plutôt que là, sa substance. [20]

Edouard never writes his novel, because his ambitious disdain of ever cutting at all is impracticable. All art is selective due to the fact that after the pages of the book there comes a cover, around a painting there is a frame, after a symphony there is silence.[21] Gide therefore had to use the scissors, and he cut in several directions and focused his flashlight at varying angles. What Edouard was suggesting, however, were the new techniques which could be applied individually. To see how they have been exploited in the modern French novel we have only to think of a work such as Michel Butor's *Degrés* where the events are seen through the varying points of view of a number of characters, or Claude Mauriac's *Le Dîner en ville* which is the description of the points of

---

[19] James, pp. 35-36.
[20] *Les Faux-Monnayeurs*, p. 232.
[21] Cf. Gide's Essay "The Limits of Art", *op. cit.*

view of eight people held together by their common experience of eating dinner, or the angles of time-perspective in a Robbe-Grillet or Beckett novel.

The disjunction of time-sequences and the combination of viewing angles, these new structural techniques of the novel, owe much to Gide's flashlight and to his scissors.

Chapter II

EDOUARD VERSUS GIDE: THE DILEMMA OF THE CRITIC

The fact that Gide widened the horizons of the novel by posing certain aesthetic problems on the art of fiction has created such a stir among the critics of *Les Faux-Monnayeurs* that theory has all but obscured the other aspects of his book. After discussing his fictional techniques it would be expedient to proceed to the very essence of the novel, but *Les Faux-Monnayeurs* has been so severely criticized for its failures, shortcomings, and abortive attempts that it is necessary, in the interest of greater objectivity, to point out certain fallacies behind premises which critics have adopted as the basis of their judgments.

Critics of such varying backgrounds as Hytier and Fowlie speak of the elusiveness of its subject matter as a perplexing source of complication. Hytier claims: "the substance to be studied appears to evaporate on analysis, so volatile is its essence by nature".[1] Fowlie finds himself in the same dilemma: "the scheme of such a novel is almost impossible to outline."[2] Brée also speaks of "la minceur de sa substance."[3] Gide states in his *Journal* that he could have been more explicit, but that he chose not to be:

> Qu'il m'eût été facile de rallier les suffrages du grand nombre en écrivant *les Faux-Monnayeurs* à la manière

---

[1] Jean Hytier, *André Gide* (New York, 1962), p. 180.
[2] Wallace Fowlie, *André Gide, His Life and Art* (New York, 1965), p. 87.
[3] Germaine Brée, *André Gide, l'Insaisissable Protée* (Paris, 1953), p. 312.

> des romans connus, décrivant les lieux et les êtres, analysant les sentiments, expliquant les situations, étalant en surface tout ce que je cache entre les phrases, et protégeant la paresse du lecteur.[4]

He asserts that there are hinted-at meanings, enigmatic but not fortuitous connections which can be found by the careful reader. Therefore, the element of failure implied by these critics directs itself against the critic rather than Gide. That *Les Faux-Monnayeurs* is a difficult novel is apparent, but this fact merely presents a greater challenge to the reader and critic to analyze it in spite of and because of those difficulties. More than the naturalist novel which claimed to be the experimental novel par excellence, this work is indeed exerimental in its use of new techniques. New techniques usually demand new methods of criticism. If our old methods cannot capture this "volatile substance," then it is perhaps time to examine not the adequacy of the novel but the adequacy of our critical methods.

Having mentioned the naturalist novel it strikes me that its influence must still be very strong in literary circles for realism to be counted among the chief virtues of novelistic achievements. Thomas Cordle for instance has said that *Les Faux-Monnayeurs* fails, because "a second-rate novelist so dwarfs and twists the characters in the story that there is little reality or life remaining in them."[5] The twofold error of which *Les Faux-Monnayeurs* stands here accused is at once the imposing reality of Edouard (since he dwarfs the others) and the lack of reality of the rest. He is therefore objecting to a lack of balance between characters which, as we have seen, was a deliberate and conscious assumption of point of view on the part of Gide. As for his deploring the absence of life-like reality, it seems almost unnecessary to point out that the degrees of realism vary with each literary school, and mimesis has run the gamut according to writer and century between the higher reality of the romantics and the stark realism of the naturalists. In fact it has been pointed out that in naturalism "literature goes about as far as a representation of life... could go

---

[4] *JAG I*, p. 938.
[5] Thomas Cordle, "Gide and the Novel of the Egoist", *Yale French Studies*, 7-8, 1951, p. 97.

and still remain literature. Beyond this point," says Frye, "the hypothetical or fictional element in literature would begin to dissolve." [6] That Gide's novel tends to weigh the scale down on the other side is evident from his unconventional use of multiple perspective.

Georges Lemaitre also infers that the realism of *Les Faux-Monnayeurs* is not satisfying to the reader. He makes essentially the same criticisms which Dhurmer makes in the novel saying that "The characters are not analysed carefully nor with any minute detail, but simply outlined like so many sketches or musical themes on which the imagination may perform endless variations. Reality is grasped not as a logical continuity but in conformity with Gide's own mental rhythm..." [7] But is reality a "logical continuity"? Life, contrary to art, is a conglomeration of illogical, discontinuous fragments. In that case what Lemaitre is really criticizing is its proximity to life. Indeed, Irvin Stock began his article on *Les Faux-Monnayeurs* with such an assumption: "If *Les Faux-Monnayeurs* is a confusing novel, the reason is that it contains more of life than any other ever written." [8] Depending on each critic's concept of mimetic values in art we have opposing views as to the measure of reality portrayed in *Les Faux-Monnayeurs*. We find ourselves involved in a circular argument from which there is no objective way to extricate ourselves.

There are very few critics who like George Painter proclaim the novel an unqualified success. [9] Apart from the completely negative critique such as Priestley's which asserted that Gide was no novelist at all, most critics convey either implicitly or explicitly that there is something wrong, unsuccessful, vaguely dissatisfying about the novel. Albérès, in his comprehensive examination of the modern novel credits Gide with having set up the schema of the modern novel, but of never having carried it out. [10] After

---

[6] Northrop Frye, *Anatomy of Criticism* (Princeton, 1957), p. 80.

[7] Georges Lemaitre, *Four French Novelists, Marcel Proust, André Gide, Jean Giraudoux, Paul Morand* (London, 1938), p. 167.

[8] Irvin Stock, "A View of Les Faux-Monnayeurs", *Yale French Studies*, 7-8, 1951, p. 72.

[9] George D. Painter, *André Gide, A Critical Biography* (London, 1968), p. 88.

[10] R.-M. Albérès, *Histoire du Roman Moderne* (Paris, 1962), p. 160.

quoting the passage from the novel where Edouard speaks of his ambition to put everything into his novel Albérès claims:

> Tout c'est beaucoup dire, et il entre en fin de compte peu de chose dans Les Faux-Monnayeurs, simplement l'incongru et le hasard, les réflexions d'un théoricien heureusement ironique. [11]

It is amazing how many critics have criticized Les Faux-Monnayeurs by Edouard's standards. By applying Edouard's statements about the novel in general to this novel in particular they have condemned the work. It is as though Gide had placed Edouard into his novel to supply the critic with a whole arsenal of weapons to be turned against him. Since most of the negative remarks aimed at Les Faux-Monnayeurs take up Edouard's theories and proceed to show us how Gide does not succeed in practice, I should think it appropriate to first ask ourselves the question whether we are not violating the very essence of critical logic when we do so. On the twenty-ninth of October, 1929, Gide was incensed enough to state in his *Journal*:

> "Je n'ai jamais rien pu inventer." C'est par une telle phrase du *Journal d'Edouard* que je pensais le mieux me séparer d'Edouard, le distinguer... Et c'est de cette phrase au contraire que l'on se sert pour prouver que, "incapable d'invention," c'est moi que j'ai peint dans Edouard et que je ne suis pas romancier. [12]

Like Albérès most critics engage in this kind of criticism without explicitly discussing whether Edouard is Gide or not. They just assume that Gide is using Edouard to be his mouthpiece. Guerard, more cautious, brings up the problem in parentheses to say merely that a "complete identification" of the two is not justified. He quickly adds, however, that "it goes without saying that Gide did see much of himself in Edouard, and often spoke through him." [13] Fowlie surprisingly claims that "Edouard is not Gide but a portrait of what Gide would have liked to have been and what he

---
[11] Albérès, pp. 159-160.
[12] *JAG I*, p. 949.
[13] Albert J. Guerard, *André Gide* (New York, 1963), p. 168.

was potentially."[14] I can agree that Gide put himself into his characters, as every artist does, but I cannot believe that Edouard represented an ideal to Gide. Apart from the clear distinction already made between Gide's and Edouard's perspective in the chapter on structural problems in the novel, there is too much evidence in the story and plot against this assumption to ever assert that Gide would have liked to become Edouard.

It is my contention, rather, that Gide, as a novelist, and Edouard, as his character-novelist, stand in direct contrast to each other. Edouard's profession and the fact that he intends to write a novel on the same subject are the only real bonds between them. Edouard may express in theory that he shies away from realism in the novel, but he seeks it in practice, for he does not really invent the conflicts which absorb his characters, he waits for reality to happen. Gide is just the opposite and has created the situations and characters including Edouard and his dilemma.

More important their views on the novel as a genre stand in complete opposition to each other. The earliest statement Gide made on the novel is the following:

> Le roman doit prouver à présent qu'il peut être autre chose qu'un miroir promené le long du chemin — qu'il peut être supérieur et *à priori* — c'est-à-dire déduit, c'est-à-dire composé, c'est-à-dire oeuvre d'art.[15]

Let us compare this statement with Edouard's in the novel:

> C'est le miroir qu'avec moi je promène. Rien de ce qui m'advient ne prend pour moi d'existence réelle, tant que je ne l'y vois pas reflété.[16]

The artistic creation depends upon Gide, whereas Edouard depends upon his art. The second pronouncement on the novel that Gide makes is to be found in his *Projet de préface pour Isabelle*:

---

[14] Fowlie, p. 93.
[15] Quoted by Jean Delay, *La Jeunesse d'André Gide* II, (Paris, 1957), p. 666. The excerpt is from an unpublished page of his *Journal* dated October 1894.
[16] *Les Faux-Monnayeurs*, p. 197.

> Le roman, tel que je le reconnais ou l'imagine, comporte une diversité de points de vue, soumise à la diversité des personnages qu'il met en scène; c'est par essence une oeuvre déconcentrée. Il m'importe du reste beaucoup moins d'en formuler la théorie que d'en écrire.[17]

This definition of the novel applies perfectly to *Les Faux-Monnayeurs* which Gide writes, but which Edouard seems incapable of completing, because of the very fact that he is too busy formulating his theories. He says for example: "A vrai dire, du livre même, je n'ai pas encore écrit une ligne."[18] and "Oui, si je ne parviens pas à l'écrire, ce livre, c'est que l'histoire du livre m'aura plus intéressé que le livre lui-même..."[19]

Another example of the difference between Gide and Edouard is again Gide's concept of the novel as an *a priori* experience composed before its actual experience.

> Le roman prouvera qu'il peut peindre autre chose que la réalité — directement l'émotion et la pensée; il montrera jusqu'à quel point il peut être déduit, *avant l'expérience des choses*...[20]

Knowing as we do from Gide's *Journal des Faux-Monnayeurs* that Gide took the example of Boris's death from a *fait divers* which actually happened at the Lycée Clermont-Ferrand it became an *a priori* dénouement for the novel he was to write. This is not true for Edouard who says he will not use Boris's death in his novel:

> Je consens que la réalité vienne à l'appui de ma pensée, comme une preuve; mais non point qu'elle la précède. Il me déplaît d'être surpris. Le suicide de Boris m'apparaît comme une *indécence*, car je ne m'y attendais pas.[21]

In addition Gide brings up the subject of Edouard in his *Journal des Faux-Monnayeurs* and shows how careful he was to portray him different from himself:

---

[17] "Projet de Préface pour Isabelle", *OC VI*, p. 361.
[18] *Les Faux-Monnayeurs*, p. 234.
[19] *Les Faux-Monnayeurs*, p. 235.
[20] Quoted by Jean Delay, II, p. 666.
[21] *Les Faux-Monnayeurs*, p. 491.

> Chaque fois qu'Edouard est appellé à exposer le plan de son roman, il en parle d'une manière différente. Somme tout, il bluffe: il craint, au fond, de ne pouvoir jamais en sortir. [22]

And:

> Je dois respecter soigneusement en Edouard tout ce qui fait qu'il ne peut écrire son livre. [23]

To apply an author's own principles of creation such as an author supplies in a critical work (as for instance Gide's *Journal des Faux-Monnayeurs*), as a yardstick of his success or failure is improper, because the measurement obtained will show merely to what extent the author was himself aware of the structural techniques he employed. To apply the principles of creation which are expounded by a character in the work to the work itself is preposterous, because the results prove merely how much or how little that particular character is like his creator, but show absolutely nothing about the intrinsic merits or demerits of the work. I surmise that had Edouard expressed in theory exactly what Gide achieved in practice the critics would have been content. This, however, would have impoverished the novel thematically, since Edouard, as we shall see in the detailed analysis of his motivations, is really another counterfeiter among counterfeiters. In spite of all his ambiguities and self-contradictions and perhaps because of them Gide has never been accused of being counterfeit.

When the criticism is aimed at Gide's inability to bring the themes of the novel to life it becomes more serious. Enid Starkie says:

> *Les Faux-Monnayeurs* is a *tour de force* in a very difficult and complicated technique, and it does not quite come off. This is largely because the separate themes are treated more slightly than is necessary, though to treat them fully would have required a novel of unprecedented length. [24]

---

[22] "Journal des Faux-Monnayeurs", *OC XIII*, p. 38.

[23] *Ibid.*, p. 42.

[24] Enid Starkie, "André Gide", *Studies in Modern French Literature* (New Haven, 1960), p. 195.

She accuses and excuses in the same breath; yet she was not the only critic to feel this way. Carlos Lynes speaks of the lack of integration of themes and continues by stating that the disconcerting and even irritating impression made by *Les Faux-Monnayeurs* is Gide's failure to "follow through" on the themes he sets into motion. [25] If true, the absence of thematic unity is a serious charge and undermines the whole essence of the work's artistic value.

Although disconcerted by its cool reception in so many circles, Gide never gave in to the temptation to explain its deeper coherence which he nevertheless persistently declared to be there. He said: "Mon livre achevé, je tire la barre et laisse au lecteur le soin de l'opération: addition, soustraction, peu importe: j'estime que ce n'est pas à moi de la faire." [26] He kept his promise and never so much as suggested interpretations to an eager critic. The few times that he mentioned his work later on in his *Journals* it was to express what he had stated before on so many other occasions when he felt his work was not being properly evaluated: "Je n'écris que pour ceux qui comprennent à demi-mot." [27] "Je n'écris que pour être relu." [28] "Le livre exige une lenteur de lecture et une méditation que l'on n'accorde à l'ordinaire pas aussitôt." [29] He literally begs us to read between the lines.

On the surface the themes of the novel may appear arbitrary, fortuitous, and seem to lead nowhere. But a novel like this cannot be read only on the surface, nor can it be read only once if we are to discern an underlying texture of meaning. In fact it cannot be read simply from beginning to end, but textually separated episodes and incidents must be seen in relation to each other. The serious reservations that Starkie, Lynes, and others have raised are valid only if we surmise that unity of structure depends solely upon sequential and causal coherence, that is story and plot. The conventional or traditional novel achieves unity by emphasizing consistency and contiguity in the construction of story and plot.

---

[25] Carlos Lynes, "André Gide and the Problem of Form in the Novel", *Forms of Modern Fiction*, op. cit., p. 185.
[26] "Journal des Faux-Monnayeurs", *OC XIII*, p. 61.
[27] *JAG I*, p. 992.
[28] "Journal des Faux-Monnayeurs", *OC XIII*, p. 28.
[29] *JAG I*, p. 991.

Les Faux-Monnayeurs is neither conventional nor traditional. Since plot and story continuity are underemphasized the integration of themes depends on the added dimension achieved by the use of various leitmotifs and by the repetition of themes in generic relationships. To appreciate this added dimension, and indeed to prove that it exists at all, a critical method must be applied to this novel which not only provides definitions of leitmotifs, of generic unity, and of the bases for linear and causal unity, but which also includes a means of detecting the function of cohesive factors within the work while respecting their dependence on textual elements.

CHAPTER III

THE INTEGRITY OF THE WORK OF ART:
THEMATIC ANALYSIS AS A CRITICAL METHOD

Philip Thody asserts in his article " 'Les Faux-Monnayeurs': the Theme of Responsibility" that *"Les Faux-Monnayeurs* has, in its plot, a much greater unity than has often been suggested' [1] and proceeds to analyze the main unifying element as the theme of responsibility which is primarily related to the fact that most of the characters must share the responsibility for Boris's death in the end. "It is an act which was planned by some people, but for which the carelessness, blindness and stupidity of others were equally responsible." [2]

It is significant that Thody affirms that there is more "unity than has often been suggested" in *Les Faux-Monnayeurs* and that he seeks to establish that unity on the thematic level. By limiting his analysis, however, to the theme of responsibility, and only to responsibility in relationship to Boris's death, he can prove the basic coherence of the novel only by virtue of that one theme. The evaluation of the other themes in the novel and how they, as individual threads of the novel, are woven into a coherent tapestry remains to be made.

Before we can begin a systematic thematic analysis of *Les Faux-Monnayeurs* it is essential to describe thematic analysis as a critical method. For the theoretical evaluation and exposition of thematic

---

[1] Philip Thody, "'Les Faux-Monnayeurs': The Theme of Responsibility", *Modern Language Review*, vol. 55, July 1960, p. 352.
[2] Thody, p. 353.

analysis I shall adopt Eugene H. Falk's method as expounded in his book *Types of Thematic Structure*.[3]

Every critical method must adopt basic criteria and principles of judgment which involve the critic's philosophy of artistic and aesthetic value. Within this framework Falk's philosophy of criticism is centripetal and seeks its aesthetic qualities within the artistic creation itself. The work of art itself is the source for analysis and furnishes intrinsically the elements on which his critical evaluation is based.

In Falk's objective approach the phenomenon of the work of art is autonomous and can be divorced from the author's biography, his philosophy of literature, as well as from his intention in writing the book. If, upon analysis of elements within the book, a "philosophy" of the author becomes evident it will have arisen out of the interior makeup of the work and will serve to corroborate or question what we already know about the author's thought. It is, in fact, quite conceivable that a work of art may reveal enlightening insights to the critic of which the author was not even aware during the creative process. Valéry remarked: "L'oeuvre dure en tant qu'elle est capable de paraître tout autre que son auteur l'avait faite."[4]

Within this world of the work of art itself Falk defines two elements which will serve as our fundamental tools of thematic analysis. They are "theme" and "motif." The basic unit of literary criticism is the "motif" which is the textual element that carries the "theme." By "theme" Falk designates the idea or ideas which can be derived from the "motifs," whereas such themes must be distinguished from the concept of theme as a generalization divorced from the motif structure which Falk calls topic. The "motifs" are "textual elements as actions, statements revealing states of mind or feelings, gestures, or meaningful environmental settings."[5] The first step of thematic analysis is therefore a simple identification of the motifs as objects, actions, and moods and corresponds to the term Falk borrows from the visual arts — a pre-iconographical evaluation.

---

[3] Eugene H. Falk, *Types of Thematic Structure* (Chicago, 1967).
[4] Paul Valéry, *Tel Quel* I (Paris, 1941), p. 168.
[5] Falk, p. 5.

To remain a moment within the context of the visual arts we ascertain readily that a work of art cannot be evaluated unless the individual motifs are seen and recognized. Such an evaluation involves a dissection of the work into its integral parts. It is immediately apparent that the second step of iconographical evaluation must involve a reunification of the separate motifs along with the themes they carry into the entire context of the work. This second procedure requires us to step back and view the whole picture from a vantage point where the separate details are subordinated to the unity of the entire painting. This "critical distanciation" is essential in the evaluation of the literary work as well, and awareness of structural coherence affords an intellectual pleasure quite distinct from the emotional involvement we may derive from enjoying a good book at the first reading. La Bruyère's statement on the work of art and the critic holds true: "Le plaisir de la critique nous ôte celui d'être vivement touchés de très belles choses." [6] There is a distinction between "plaisir de la critique" and "être touché" and the critic is aware that the studied analysis of the work of art sacrifices the pleasure of emotion to the pleasure of knowledge.

To see the structural coherence of a painting is to appreciate the compositional elements which are part of the work of art. Transposed to the poem in its vastest meaning beauty, in Aristotelean terms, depends upon size and order and upon an "action which is whole and complete." [7] Unity and coherence are therefore the basic aesthetic principles we must consider and Falk distinguishes between three types of coherence: the linear or sequential coherence based on the story, the causal or generative coherence based on the plot, [8] and the generic coherence based on an affinity of themes regardless of their textual disposition.

The *linear coherence* leads the reader from one incident to the next in a course prescribed by the author's intention of telling his story. In this linear sequence incidents follow each other in an order of *probability* whereas *transposal* of one incident in the

---

[6] Jean de La Bruyère, "Des Ouvrages de l'Esprit", *Les Caractères*, 20 (1) (Paris, 1962), p. 72.

[7] Aristotle, *On Poetry and Style,* trans. G. M. A. Grube (New York, 1958), p. 16.

[8] For the definition of story and plot see Chapter one, p. 24.

story to another place will destroy its linear coherence. Probability is based on the incidents being related to each other in a sequential order where one incident is conceived as the antecedent of the next, but where that antecedent incident has no generative effect on the following incident.[9] The author's technique, however, in telling the story may vary. He may use flashbacks and interruptions and may even begin his story at the end and fill in the background. This does not hinder us from being able to establish the linear progression of the story.

Practically, the linear coherence of the story is based on our recognition of the motifs of the incidents of the story and our abstraction of their individual themes, whereas "incidents in the story" are not only actions, their course and outcome, but also character relationships, the physical, intellectual, and moral environment in which they move, and elements of change which affect both characters and situations.[10] The thematic significance of each incident is viewed in relationship to the total sequential structure of the work.

Causal coherence is based on the generative forces behind the incidents; it emanates from the characters' motivations and purposes which cause and give impetus to their deeds. In establishing the causal coherence of a work we seek to find the cause-effect relationships behind the various incidents which constitute the plot. These incidents are governed by the *necessity* of one incident generating the next, whereby *withdrawal* of one incident will upset the causal coherence. Therefore, when we seek the themes of the plot we are establishing the forces within the work itself which instigate and sustain actions. These forces are motivations and purposes which "(1) bring about the coherence of actions in the structure of the plot, (2) explain the origin and direction of actions and (3) invest the actions with the meanings they have — not as mere symptoms of these forces, but as effects thereof."[11]

In summary, the recognition of the motifs of the story in the pre-iconographical stage leads to the interpretation of their meaning on the iconographical level where we derive universal qualities

---

[9] Falk, p. 5.
[10] Falk, p. 24.
[11] Falk, p. 27.

from the sequence of incidents which constitute the themes of the story. The recognition of the motifs of the plot which leads to the interpretation of their meaning on the iconological level (whereas the forces behind the actions are contained within the work itself) is expressed by motivations and purposes which constitute the themes of the plot.

The third kind of coherence in the work of art is what Falk calls "generic coherence" and consists of a reciprocal relatedness of themes. It is the search for this reciprocal relatedness of themes which often proves to be the most challenging and rewarding quest in thematic analysis. Repeated readings result in the discovery of unexpected relationships on the thematic level where motifs, regardless of the sequential order or causal relationship in which they occur, are related thematically either by contrast or similarity. Hence themes which can be found to be related to each other in a generic sense are *correlative themes* and the motif clusters which carry them are named *component motifs*.

Falk distinguishes between two groups of component motifs, the component motifs which are not *leitmotifs* and those that are. In the first instance the component motifs which are not leitmotifs establish a parallelism between at least two incidents of the text, whereby the parallel component motifs may be materially similar or materially different.[12] Materially similar component motifs quite naturally point to the same theme. To take an obvious example from *Les Faux-Monnayeurs* we can state that, in spite of differing circumstances, both Olivier and Bernard leave home. The incidents of each boy's actual departure constitute parallel component motifs which carry the correlative theme of separation from a former environment. The events which lead up to each boy's departure are materially different component motifs which, however, express the same thing on the thematic level, namely that youth seeks to break the chains of a past establishment. These parallelisms between the two boys contribute to the generic coherence of the novel, but as such do not constitute what Falk calls leitmotifs which belong to the second group of component motifs.

---

[12] Falk, p. 16.

This second group of component motifs accomplishes much the same task in the literary work as leitmotifs in a musical composition. In speaking of Wagner's use of leitmotifs Donald Grout says that they are "musical labels" which accumulate significance as they recur in new contexts. A leitmotif may "serve to recall the thought of its object in situations where the object itself is not present; it may be varied or developed in accord with the development of the plot; similarity of motifs may suggest an underlying connection between the objects to which they refer; motifs may be contrapuntally combined; and, finally, repetition of motifs is an effective means of musical unity." [13]

In transposing the term from music to literature Falk has defined three types of leitmotifs according to their nature and function. They are the repetitious label, the linking phrase, and the linking image.

The repetitious label may be a gesture, a word, or a phrase whose basic function is to emphasize some "particular trait of a character." [14] The repetition of the same phrasing in a new situation calls our attention to correlative themes and is called a linking phrase. Not only words or phrases, but a whole image can be repeated by the artist for the purpose of relating themes. The image thus repeated becomes a linking image and is usually placed focally in the text "so that its diverging rays reach situations in the text and so that themes carried by these situations converge upon it." [15]

Let us examine instances of the application of these three terms in order to illustrate their meaning. In the second chapter of *Les Faux-Monnayeurs* Gide uses the repetitious label to refer to Albéric Profitendieu's liver ailment:

> ...il s'inquiétait de sentir une certaine pesanteur au côté droit; la fatigue, chez lui, portait sur le foie... (p. 15) [16]

---

[13] Donald Jay Grout, *A History of Western Music* (New York, 1960), p. 564.
[14] Falk, p. 9.
[15] Falk, p. 15.
[16] All quotations from *Les Faux-Monnayeurs* are from the Gallimard edition, 1925.

> ...il ressentait un petit pincement au côté droit, là, sous les côtes; il n'y couperait pas: c'était la crise de foie. (pp. 24-25)

> ...d'une voix plaintive, quasi suppliante, car la colique hépatique commençait à le faire cruellement souffrir... (p. 25)

Then Gide emphasizes the pain by adding the moral suffering caused by Bernard's departure:

> Sa douleur au côté se confond avec sa tristesse, la prouve et la localise. Il lui semble qu'il a du chagrin au foie. (p. 25)

The burden of the family crisis weighs heavily on Profitendieu and expresses itself in the acute pain in his right side. After his first lie about Bernard's absence the pain begins to subside; the first step to cope with the situation has been taken:

> Profitendieu se sentait mieux. Il avait d'abord eu peur d'être trop souffrant pour pouvoir parler. (p. 28)

As his wife is reading Bernard's letter:

> Il ne songe plus à son mal. Il la suit des yeux, tout le long de la lettre, ligne après ligne. Tout à l'heure en parlant, il avait peine à retenir ses larmes; à présent l'émotion même l'abandonne... (p. 29)

In contrast now to Profitendieu's earlier pain-ridden posture which was reinforced by the burden of facing the immediate dilemma of the crisis Profitendieu literally rises to the occasion as his wife in turn cannot cope with the situation. The significance of the scene is enhanced by the cumulative effect of the description of his earlier pain and attitude, and therefore the preceding repetitious label has served to emphasize the contrast. Profitendieu is a changed person:

> Il s'est levé, par instinctif besoin de dominer; il se tient à présent tout dressé, oublieux et insoucieux de sa douleur physique, et pose gravement, tendrement, autoritairement la main sur l'épaule de Marguerite. (p. 30)

The repetitious label has served to emphasize Profitendieu's characteristic feature. We realize through Gide's ingenious selectivity of incidents that Profitendieu is a man quickly disconcerted by a conflict with which he cannot cope, and that he is as quickly cured of his malaise as soon as he controls the situation, as soon as he can recapture his dominant pose. We shall not encounter him again in the novel until he comes to see Edouard, ostensibly about Georges, but in reality about Bernard. Again we witness a parallel transformation. As earlier the physical pain changed to moral suffering soon to be overshadowed by his almost involuntary need to pass judgment, we witness in this parallel incident the crushed, self-denying affection of the father change into the self-confident officiousness of the judge. Profitendieu's initial difficulty in speech is emphasized by repeated interpolations on the part of Edouard such as "Il respirait péniblement entre chaque phrase" and "puis d'une voix qui faiblissait" to "il ne put achever" (p. 427). Similar to the "crise de foie" in the second chapter the difficulty of speech is soon cancelled out by the emergence of his heightened stature as judge. Let us compare the two passages in juxtaposition:

> Il s'est levé par instinctif besoin de dominer; il se tient à présent tout dressé, oublieux et insoucieux de sa douleur physique, et pose gravement, tendrement, autoritairement la main sur l'épaule de Marguerite. (p. 30)

Edouard has just mentioned the piece of counterfeit money:

> Je ne lui eus pas plus tôt parlé de celle-ci que Profitendieu changea de visage; ses paupières se fermèrent à demi, tandis qu'au fond de ses yeux s'allumait une flamme bizarre; sur ses tempes, la patte d'oie se marqua; ses lèvres se pincèrent; l'attention tira vers en haut tous ses traits. De tout ce qu'il m'avait dit d'abord, il ne fut plus question. Le juge envahissait le père, et rien plus n'existait pour lui que le métier. (p. 429)

The juxtaposition of these two passages shows the correlation of themes carried by materially different component motifs. The final significance of this parallelism resides in the comparative importance of the theme they express within the entire context of the work. These two episodes concerning Profitendieu do not really place him in an unfavorable light, but illustrate that his stature as a man is in direct relationship to the rôle he occupies in society. He is inadequate apart from the rôle he has assumed; he is no longer a person but a function of his office and therefore belongs to the long line of those who are among the counterfeit. By recognizing a repetitious label we have been led to see a dominant feature of a character. By noticing its use in a new and contrasting situation we have gone beyond the mere repetitious label to an important theme of the entire novel, and we have seen that theme reconfirmed in a subsequent passage.

When component motifs are textually far apart a recurring wording or phrasing may call our attention to their correlation. This is what Falk calls the linking phrase. "The primary function of the repetitious label," he says, "is to emphasize the theme it itself carries — a theme descriptive of character, whereas the primary function of a recurring linking phrase is to allude by its recurrence to the similarity or the contrast of themes in connection with which it appears in sequentially separated situations." [17]

Three completely separate incidents in *Les Faux-Monnayeurs* which involve different characters are thus related by a striking resemblance of phrasing. Vincent is pondering the dilemma he is in because of his illicit affair with Laura:

> Son aventure avec Laura lui paraissait, suivant les heures du jour, ou monstrueuse ou toute naturelle. Il suffit, bien souvent, de *l'addition d'une quantité de petits faits très simples et très naturels,* chacun pris à part, pour obtenir un *total monstrueux.* (p. 49; my italics)

In Edouard's Journal we read about his second visit to the La Pérouse household. Madame La Pérouse opens the door and takes advantage of Edouard's presence to enumerate various irritating details about her husband's behavior:

> La vieille, à coup sur, n'inventait rien; je comprenais, à travers son récit, que l'interprétation *de menus gestes innocents seule leur conférait* une signification offensante, et *quelle ombre monstrueuse* la réalité projetait sur la paroi de cet étroit cerveau. (p. 199; my italics)

---

[17] Falk, p. 12.

And to find a similar link to the preceding passages let us quote Strouvilhou, who, in his typical fashion, denounces humanity and uses similar phrasing, this time twisted negatively:

> Quant à moi, je prétends que s'il y a quelque chose de plus méprisable que l'homme, et de plus abject, c'est beaucoup d'hommes. Aucun raisonnement ne saurait me convaincre que *l'addition d'unités sordides puisse donner un total exquis*. (p. 411; my italics)

The consequences derived from these various instances take on their notable significance when we analyze what these component motifs are expressing on the thematic level. First, they express the existential tenet that we are the sum total of our acts and that even the most innocent incident of our lives contributes to the total picture. Hence all our acts are interrelated, not only on an individual basis, but also collectively as each affects the entire human race. In the "distanciated" perspective of the whole work we can appreciate the thematic significance of the sentence: "il suffit, bien souvent, de l'addition d'une quantité de petits faits très simples et très naturels, chacun pris à part, pour obtenir un total monstrueux" (p. 49), for the "total monstrueux" which Gide illustrates most vividly is the tragedy of Boris's suicide-murder. This thematic interpretation is in turn confirmed by Edouard's parenthetic statement on the novel:

> (et toute oeuvre d'art n'est que *la somme ou le produit des solutions d'une quantité de menues difficultés successives*). (p. 235; italics mine)

The linking image differs from the linking phrase by nature not function. Instead of depending on wording and phrasing it depends on its perceptual portrayal of a theme. The very first incident in the book relates how Bernard found the love letters:

> Il remit la liasse dans le coffret et le coffret dans le tiroir de la console. Le tiroir n'était pas ouvert; il avait livré son secret par en haut. Bernard assujettit les lames disjointes du plafond de bois, que devait recouvrir une lourde plaque d'onyx. Il fit doucement, précautionneusement, retomber celle-ci, replaça par-dessus deux candélabres de cristal et l'encombrante pendule qu'il venait de s'amuser à réparer. (p. 8)

The theme this incident conveys is the discovery of the secret of his birth by lifting off the marble top of the console. The implication of the theme points to the fact that the more sordid secrets of the family are carefully covered by the guise of respectability. Within the incident itself the marble-top table becomes an image for the cautious concealment of an unwanted reality which was literally hidden under the weight of time. This image is reinforced later when Bernard reflects on what he has done:

> Dire que si je n'avais pas forcé ce tiroir, j'aurais pu croire toute ma vie que je nourrissais à l'égard d'un père des sentiments dénaturés... (p. 73)
>
> Thésée devait avoir mon âge quand il souleva le rocher. Ce qui empêche pour le guéridon, d'ordinaire, c'est la pendule. Je n'aurais pas songé à soulever la plaque de marbre du guéridon si je n'avais pas voulu réparer la pendule.... Ce qui n'arrive pas à n'importe qui, c'est de trouver là-dessous des armes; ou des lettres d'un amour coupable. (p. 74)

This parallel passage serves to reinforce the importance of the image, the comparison with Theseus stresses the actual meaning for young Bernard. The significance, however, for the thematic development of the novel becomes evident when we read the following in Edouard's Journal:

> Certes, il n'est pas de geôle (intellectuelle) dont un vigoureux esprit ne s'échappe; et rien de ce qui pousse à la révolte n'est définitivement dangereux — encore que la révolte puisse fausser le caractère (elle le replie, le retourne ou le cabre et conseille une ruse impie); et l'enfant qui ne cède pas à l'influence familiale, use à s'en délivrer la primeur de son énergie. (p. 142)
>
> ...la réalité m'intéresse comme une matière plastique; et j'ai plus de regard pour ce qui pourrait être, infiniment plus que pour ce qui a été. Je me penche vertigineusement sur les possibilités de chaque être et pleure tout ce que le couvercle des moeurs atrophie. (p. 144)

The "couvercle des moeurs" reminds us of the marble-top which covered the Profitendieu family secret. In turn the "couvercle des moeurs" leads to other threads in the thematic fabric. It invites comparison with the numerous instances of such a stifling influence in the novel, and the motif of the hidden love letters corresponds to the motif of the found diary of Pasteur Vedel which reveals his secret passion, as well as Oscar Molinier's love letters, also hidden away in some secret drawer, though not impervious to Georges' snooping curiosity. As we shall discover in the themes of the plot even Edouard's Journal unwittingly reveals his secrets. The simple image of the marble-top table has led us to the center of the novel, for it soon appears that many of the characters have a "skeleton" hidden away in their respective closets, and that one of their chief concerns is to cover up their aberrations by appearances of conventionality which are only surface manifestations and are quickly peeled off like so many layers on an onion. The unmasking of the real nature of the characters, their exposure for what they really are, the raising of the "couvercle des moeurs" constitutes one of the central themes of the novel. Thus even the most insignificant image, which at first appears merely peripheral, leads us over numerous relationships to the very core of the novel.

In discussing the basic unity which is an aesthetic necessity of the work of art we have borrowed the terms iconography and iconology from the visual arts and the concept of leitmotifs from music. The distinction between the verbal epic and the visual arts, their respective limitations and advantages, as expounded in Lessing's *Laokoön*, is the difference in the time element needed to perceive each genre's essential unity. Whereas the visual arts are limited to the "fruchtbarer Augenblick" of expression but have the advantage of simultaneous impact, the literary work is forced by textual concreteness to fall into a sequential order of successive moments in time. Music is similarly limited by the time element of perception, but is able to achieve simultaneity of expression by the use of counterpoint. What counterpoint is to music, the generic coherence of themes is to literature.

The scope of *Les Faux-Monnayeurs* is vast. A novel of more than forty characters which, in addition to telling their individual stories, questions, evaluates, and discusses the novel and explores its possibilities as a genre would by its very size threaten to disintegrate into episodic tableaux were it not for Gide's effort of composition which successfully exploits the added dimension of generic unity. The novel itself contains the clue to generic coherence when Gide has Edouard expound his theory on the novel:

> Ce que je voudrais faire, comprenez-moi, c'est quelque chose qui serait comme *L'Art de la Fugue*. Et je ne vois pas pourquoi ce qui fut possible en musique, serait impossible en littérature. (p. 237)

The fascinating quality of the fugue is its capacity to relate themes in a contrapuntal arrangement. It is one of the most rigorous musical forms, because it demands a simultaneous exposition of multiple themes along with purity and an almost mathematical precision. Transposed to literature we might say that Gide accomplishes for the novel what Bach achieved for the fugue.

Thematic analysis thus deals with both content and form as it seeks out the thematic content of the individual motifs and relates them to each other in the entire structural coherence of the novel. As Falk explains, the superiority of the narrative to what it depicts lies in the perspective opened up on the various coherences, a perspective which the customary discontinuity of our daily lives seldom affords.[18] The superiority of Falk's critical method lies in its presuppositionless approach to each work of art. It lets us appraise each literary work with regard for its individuality and inherent aesthetic qualities. Its outstanding feature is its deep respect for the integrity of the artistic creation.

---

[18] Falk, p. 8.

CHAPTER IV

IDENTITY AND DESTINY:
CENTRAL THEMES OF THE STORY

One of the main themes expressed by the incidents in the story is the critical development of the young and their desire to escape. "Rien n'est plus difficile à observer que les êtres en formation" (p. 110), says Edouard. Bernard and Olivier both escape from their milieu for a while and return to it, wiser if not untainted by their experiences. Like in a *Bildungsroman* the young friends have encountered life from both sides: Olivier has gone on an adventure of debauch and luxury into Passavant's pseudo-intellectual world and has returned to Edouard's unfailing affection after which he attempts to commit suicide; Bernard has gone to the more ascetic Saas-Fée where after conceiving an idealized love for Laura he returns from his mountaintop experience to the drab atmosphere of the Vedel pension where he makes love to Sarah and then returns home to his father. From an atmosphere of unreality Bernard progresses toward what he conceives of as "probité" and "authenticité" and in so doing is far more realistic than Edouard of whom he asks counsel. At the end of the novel the recognition of the consequences of his acts leads him to maturity in that he is now ready to assume the responsibility for his actions and return to his father's house.

Georges, the sophisticated *lycéen*, met stealing a book is involved in two gangs and escapes all parental control until the suicide of Boris brings him back to the parental fold. Armand, whose family wanted him to become a pastor, cannot escape like his older brother, Alexandre, to some distant idyl on the Cassamance, but remains in the dreariest room in the whole pension, as he himself says, a schizoid observer of his own actions. Boris escapes his mother's world through his magic, Madame Sophroniska's world through Bronja, and the world of the pension through suicide. Sarah escapes her puritanical background by purposely provoking situations with immoral overtones. Laura also tries to escape her conventional marriage by running away after her illicit affair, but she also returns to her husband's arms. Among all these young people Rachel is the exception which confirms the rule. But even she escapes into the world of her own self-renunciation and her physical blindness.

For the young people of the novel the theme can be stated as follows: Youth seeks to break the chains which imprison it under the authority of a past establishment, but once the chains are broken they are perplexed with the prospect of their own freedom, their dependence upon others to maintain it, and its consequences. They search for an ideal to follow and most often find that they have gone astray only to be able to return to the fold. Hence one of the central themes of the story expressed by the actual outcome of the incidents is resignation and acceptance. The young have experienced their moment of rebellion and are forced by circumstances beyond their immediate control to adopt a basic attitude toward life.

Among the middle-aged in the novel the central theme of resignation is continued. Albéric Profitendieu is resigned to his rôle in life, to his wife's momentary infidelity, even to accepting someone else's son as his own. Pauline is resigned, even though she rebels against being "raisonnable", to the fact that she cannot even show her affection to her own sons. She is resigned to the fact that Oscar and her sons sense the need to dissimulate in front of her. She says: "On ne demandait pourtant pas beaucoup de la vie. On apprend à en demander moins encore ...toujours moins" (p. 348). Edouard himself is almost middle-aged and enjoys life only vicariously through the very young. Once the peregrinations of the young reach a static level of development Edouard turns his attention to the younger Profitendieu boy, Caloub, whose development he will now observe.

As for the aged of the novel a dimension of the tragic is portrayed which is all the more poignant, because the old no longer have the opportunity to change. They must reconcile themselves to the essence they have accepted as their own without realizing that this was not their true destiny. With this distinct impression of his failure, of having been duped, Monsieur La Pérouse's existence becomes a meaningless struggle between his desire to die and his failure to have the courage to kill himself. On the surface his struggle seems to be resolved when his only link with life, his grand-son Boris, dies, and he can enjoy the silence of subdued resignation once again. The old Azaïs is just as pitiful as he looks upon the young people around him, understanding them so little when he thinks he understands them so well. His outlook on life is typical of the blindness that convictions about the absolute produce. His very intransigence invites Georges' lies about his "petit club enfantin." As Edouard puts it: "L'éblouissement de leur foi les aveugle sur le monde qui les entoure, et sur eux-mêmes" (p. 134).

Every age of life is thus represented in *Les Faux-Monnayeurs* and we soon realize that Gide places all humanity in front of the same dilemma. Man sets out to solve the problems of reality and ends up resigned to the inevitable lack of any absolute solution. Reality is elusive, and even Edouard, the theoretician, cannot grasp it. Bernard realizes this when he pulls out the piece of counterfeit money that he has received from the grocer:

> Mais maintenant que vous l'avez examinée, rendez-la-moi!
> Je vois, hélas! que la réalité ne vous intéresse pas.
> —Si, dit Edouard; mais elle me gêne. (p. 240)

The novel is not just a story of forty individuals as they develop and react, but also as they interact and form into groups. There is the family group which disintegrates during the course of the novel into individuals going in opposite directions. Once the young peoples' interests have turned away from family to the larger world of society they split off into social, patriotic, or literary groups or into gangs with a criminal or carnal intent. Because the members of most of these groups are unstable as individuals the groups themselves fall easy prey to a dominant character behind the scenes, such as Passavant in his manoeuvering to get a literary journal underway, or as Strouvilhou in his scheming to peddle his counterfeit money. Any given group seems to have the potential to serve or threaten society, but the actual result in *Les Faux-Monnayeurs* of this banding together into groups is the unleashing of negative and destructive forces. The dangers of collective stagnation are clearly portrayed in the conservative political party Bernard encounters, and the extreme power of collective madness leads to Boris's suicide-murder. Even in the sphere of artistic and literary endeavor the group effort has served merely to encourage insipidity and absurdity.

In the story the particular incident of counterfeiting propagated by Strouvilhou, the mastermind behind the swindle, and carried out by the group of boys, is subordinated to the universal application of values, whether it be the value of money, of an idea, or of a personality. Thus the way in which we perceive reality, the evaluation of appearances, is another theme of the story. Edouard, as the novelist, writing the book of the same title, claims the real subject of his work is the struggle between the reality presented by the facts and an ideal reality. This ideal reality becomes unattainable as he is constantly expounding his theory on a novel he is never able to write. The act of being creative, however, of actually producing a work of art, of being an artist in the world of conflicting realities, is the pervasive theme of the novel, theme as topic, and makes *Les Faux-Monnayeurs* in a very real sense a *Künstlerroman*. Inasmuch as Edouard's vacillation in between his idealistic concepts and reality presents man's universal predicament Gide has transposed the dilemma of the artist to Everyman's struggle to grasp reality.

First and foremost Edouard reveals himself in his Journal, but we soon learn through Edouard himself that he cannot distinguish between reality and illusion, what he imagines he feels and what he really feels, or even if he feels anything apart from his representation of that feeling. Hence his actions speak louder than his words, and his actions portray a man who is a failure. He is caught up in the dichotomy of being actor and spectator of his deeds at the same time, and in the end seems incapable of truly living. With the exception of his relationship to Olivier, which may however prove to be transitory also, his relationships to others tend to disintegrate as soon as he realizes they exist.

He seeks to save Laura who hints at suicide and helps her out of her predicament, although we must bear in mind that it was he who advised her to marry Douviers in the first place. He also seeks to bring Boris into an affectionate relationship with his grandfather, but indirectly leads him to suicide. In his search to be creative with the "matière plastique" that is a human life he saves one person only to destroy another. Correlative by contrast are his redemptive and destructive powers.

Edouard does not have an independent personality; he is constantly being molded by those around him. His relationship to others is continuously placed in jeopardy by his need to analyze his own feelings toward them. Thus Laura has a power over him of which she is not even aware. He goes as far as to claim that without her he would not be himself:

> Il me paraît même que si elle n'était pas là pour me préciser, ma propre personnalité s'éperdrait en contours trop vagues; je ne me rassemble et ne me définis qu'autour d'elle. (p. 88)

In the course of events, however, this dependence for his own existence on another person is transposed to Olivier of whom he speaks in almost identical terms: "C'est par lui, c'est à travers lui que je sens et que je respire." (p. 422).

Edouard's relationships to others show an uncomfortable erosion of contours, a lack of anything we can pin down and define. He is an idealist, but an idealist bound by an almost slavish realism in his observations of others. Bernard, on the other hand, conceives an idealistic love for Laura, a veneration and an esteem which inspire him to a higher reality. In direct contrast to his love for Laura is his degrading passion for Sarah which he abandons in disgust once he realizes what this passion has done, not to Sarah, but to Rachel and himself. Bernard has progressed from a dangerous feeling of absolute moral freedom (his liberation from his family, his attitude toward taking Edouard's suitcase and delving into his secrets) to a feeling of extreme solitude when he realizes after successfully passing his *bachot* that he has no one with whom to share his success, to a sense of moral responsibility for what he is to become in relationship to others as well as to himself.

Olivier's relationship to others is hindered by the same paralysis we have encountered in Edouard — the impossibility to comprehend and communicate that which he really feels. He has "une singulière incapacité de jauger son crédit dans le coeur et l'esprit d'autrui" (p. 96). He loves Bernard, but becomes jealous of him as soon as he feels excluded. His departure with Passavant is the direct result and will be examined more closely in the themes of the plot. In the end his inhibition to show his feelings for Edouard is overcome when he is rescued by the affectionate hand of Edouard after his ostentatious and ridiculous plea for attention at the Argonaut banquet. The result of the fulfillment of his most fervent wish is the anguish he conceives that such perfect joy may never again be reached. Hence his attempted suicide paradoxically becomes the supreme expression of his love for Edouard.

At the start of the novel Bernard Profitendieu and Vincent Molinier have essentially the same potential opportunities as they face life. Their different reactions and encounters with life, however, soon lead them in opposite directions. Their destinies in the book are correlative by contrast, and Gide portrays this contrast in revealing detail. Just before Vincent compromises his future by going to spend the night with Lady Griffith he hesitates briefly:

> Vincent fit quelques pas sur le quai, traversa la Seine, gagna cette partie des Tuileries qui se trouve en dehors des grilles, s'approcha d'un petit bassin et trempa dans l'eau son mouchoir qu'il appliqua sur son front et ses tempes. Puis, lentement, il revint vers la demeure de Lilian. Laissons-le tandis que le diable amusé le regarde glisser sans bruit la petite clef dans la serrure... (p. 70)

At the same time in another part of the city Bernard is waking up:

> Dans un instant, se dit-il, j'irai vers mon destin. Quel beau mot: l'aventure! ...Debout, valeureux Bernard! Il est temps.
> Il frotte son visage d'un coin de serviette trempée; se recoiffe; se rechausse. Il ouvre la porte sans bruit. Dehors! (p. 72)

As Vincent is imprisoning himself in a diabolical relationship which will lead to his ruin, Bernard is liberating himself from all ties. He is free, outside. The very textual proximity between the two episodes lets us appreciate the contrast. Furthermore, Vincent has succumbed to his love of money which will add yet another tie to restrain his potential worth, whereas Bernard gets rid of his last two *sous* to a poor beggar in the streets.

> Charité? Défi? Peu importe. A présent, il se sent heureux comme un roi. Il n'a plus rien: tout est à lui! (p. 72)

Bernard and Vincent represent the two opposing forces in man. Bernard strives upward toward freedom; Vincent although he thinks he is freeing himself is irremediably bound to the demon that possesses him. As the narrator points out in his enumeration of the stages of transition through which Vincent passes:

> Griserie du gagnant. Dédain de la réserve. Suprématie.
> A partir de quoi, le démon a partie gagnée.
> A partir de quoi, l'être qui se croit le plus libre, n'est plus qu'un instrument à son service. (p. 179)

Unaware of the moral and spiritual bankruptcy toward which he is being led, he helps make Olivier's unfortunate departure with Passavant possible and eventually cuts himself off from his conscience so completely that he becomes capable of the act of murder. Earlier in his development there was still hope for him as his mixed emotions after his first night with Lilian attest:

> Vincent, tout en marchant, médite; il éprouve que du rassasiement des désirs peut naître, accompagnant la joie et comme s'abritant derrière elle, une sorte de désespoir. (p. 82)

In this period of transition which will ultimately lead him to the despair he had sensed earlier, the realization of the emptiness in the satisfaction of physical desire is only a vague voice which Lilian will succeed in silencing with all the magic her philosophy of life devises. In contrast, Bernard's transition from complete freedom to a sense of responsibility is brought about by a similar incident — his affair with Sarah. The potential outcome of any act may as equally lead to heaven as to hell. The good or evil lies not in the incident itself, but in the reaction we have to it.[1] Thus

---

[1] "Bernard a pris pour maxime:
Si ce n'est toi, qui le fera?

Bernard uses his debauching experience as a step to a higher morality:

> ...Bernard comprit aussitôt tout ce qu'elle [Rachel] avait à lui dire. Il ne répondit rien, courba la tête, et par grande pitié pour Rachel, soudain prit Sarah en haine et le plaisir qu'il goûtait avec elle en horreur. (p. 438)
> Bernard était grave. Sa lutte avec l'ange l'avait mûri. Il ne ressemblait déjà plus à l'insouciant voleur de valise qui croyait qu'en ce monde il suffit d'oser. Il commençait à comprendre que le bonheur d'autrui fait souvent les frais de l'audace. (p. 439)

This transition to a healthy attitude toward the highest potential of his life was foreshadowed in the book when the author stops to examine his characters. "Nous avons déjà vu Bernard changer; des passions peuvent le modifier encore" (pp. 275-76).

Laura and Lady Griffith are complementary figures to the characters of Bernard and Vincent. Both can be seen as fallen women, yet Laura has a depth of understanding which can inspire men to higher deeds, whereas Lilian lacks any depth whatsoever. Speaking of Lilian Gide says: "De tels personnages sont taillés dans une étoffe sans épaisseur" (p. 277). They seem to have everything except a soul. The traumatic experience during the shipwreck of the *Bourgogne* changed Lilian from a sensitive girl into a ruthless woman. There is no progression in her relationships to men, since she gives herself too freely for the gift to have any worth. Her love therefore turns into hatred as she writes to Passavant out of Africa: "...l'amour nous paraissant trop fade, nous avons pris le parti de nous haïr" (p. 408). How closely love and hatred are related Gide shows us in his perceptive analysis of the irrational personality of a Dostoevsky character, a subject he treated in lectures given at the Vieux-Colombier while he was in the process of writing *Les Faux-Monnayeurs*. The atmosphere surrounding Lilian Griffith is an atmosphere of intense emotion which has

---

Si pas maintenant, quand sera-ce?
...
Ces maximes ont ceci de charmant qu'elles sont aussi bien la clef du Paradis, que de l'Enfer."
"Journal des Faux-Monnayeurs", *OC XIII*, p. 39.

neither a beautiful development nor a sorrowful decline. Her death is brought about by the consistent application of her own philosophy of life.

Laura loves Edouard, but marries Douviers, experiences a brief passion with Vincent, inspires an idealistic love in Bernard and returns to her husband, richer for the experience, perhaps, but not happier. Her error in life was to have cut herself off from the future, just as Lilian's was to have cut herself off from the past.

Bernard analyzes her problem aptly when he says:

> Je crois que le secret de votre tristesse (car vous êtes triste, Laura) c'est que la vie vous a divisée; l'amour n'a voulu de vous qu'incomplète; vous répartissez sur plusieurs ce que vous auriez voulu donner à un seul. (p. 252)

She is torn between her frantic search for happiness and the reality of a mediocre substitute, and only in the end does she resign herself to the fact that the passion of her dreams does not correspond to reality, that her dream-world does not exist. Edouard is confronted with the same dichotomy between reality and illusion:

> Ce à quoi je parviens le plus difficilement à croire, c'est à ma propre réalité. Je m'échappe sans cesse et ne comprends pas bien, lorsque je me regarde agir, que celui que je vois agir soit le même que celui qui regarde, et qui s'étonne, et doute qu'il puisse être acteur et contemplateur à la fois. (p. 90)

The counterpart to this passage is Armand Vedel's analysis of the same problem. Instead of seeking to reconcile the fact that man is actor and spectator at the same time, Armand frankly admits his schizoid tendencies:

> Quoi que je dise ou fasse, toujours une partie de moi reste en arrière, qui regarde l'autre se compromettre, qui l'observe, qui se fiche d'elle et la siffle, ou qui l'applaudit. Quand on est ainsi divisé, comment veux-tu qu'on soit sincère? (pp. 464-465)

which brings us to another theme of the story, a pet preoccupation of Gide's, the theme of sincerity.

Sincerity is as elusive as reality, because if man does not really know who he is, then how can he sincerely be what he does not know himself to be? Those who act as though they were always the same are either blind or playing a comedy with lines as well rehearsed as the rapid little "phrases banales" of Pasteur Vedel, who, Edouard reflects, fears more than anything else "un peu de temps pour réfléchir". As Armand realizes his father "joue au pasteur", but then every one plays a rôle, a rôle which he either thinks is expected of him or which he expects of himself.

For months Edouard and Olivier pretend they do not love each other. All her life Pauline has been forced to play a rôle she does not want, to the point of denying herself the naturalness of showing her maternal affection. Laura realizes in the end that she must fit into the rôle of dignified wife and mother with a husband she does not love. Poor Félix Douviers sets out in the ridiculous rôle of the chivalrous knight who must challenge his rival to a duel, while Edouard discerns clearly: "...un Douviers pour être jaloux doit se figurer qu'il doit l'être" (p. 421). And Passavant is the typical example of the person who exists only in relation to the rôle he has assumed in society. As a dilettante artist Passavant describes himself best when he says: "ce que l'homme a de plus profond, c'est sa peau" (p. 328). Like the counterfeit coin which wears down to transparent crystal, Passavant's outer appearance hides only nothingness beneath.

The assumption of rôles in society makes the counterfeit personality inevitable. Never at one time can a character in *Les Faux-Monnayeurs* say absolutely what and who he is. Faced with the alternatives life offers, a balance becomes necessary between absolutes, between the extremes of complete resignation and complete rejection of life, because both extremes make life meaningless. La Pérouse's extreme resignation to the lack of human freedom is an admission of absurd meaninglessness. If he did not kill himself, he says, it is because his rôle in the comedy of life was not yet over, because the great stage-director, who is God, was not pulling the puppet strings of his life in the way the puppet had thought they would be pulled. His final resignation is an admission of defeat. On the other side of the coin Boris's final rejection of life, although admired for the courage it took, cannot be an answer either. And suicide is not the only means of rejecting life, since Boris's earlier "paresse" and his mysticism were just different manifestations of his rejection of reality.

In between the two extremes lies the acceptance of life which, however, can be just as meaningless as resignation or rejection if such acceptance is based on the blindness of a faith which allows no questions or on the blindness of a doubt which allows no answers. In the former instance an acceptance based on the blindness of a faith which allows no questions is demonstrated by Vedel and Azaïs whose religion becomes a cowardly escape from the responsibilities of life. In the latter instance, an acceptance based on the blindness of a doubt which allows no answer is demonstrated by Lilian, Vincent, Armand, and Passavant whose outlook on life also becomes a cowardly escape from life's responsibilities. In both extremes acceptance is only apparent and really serves to camouflage an underlying escapism whether they themselves are aware of it or not.

Edouard strives toward total awareness in order to base his attitude toward life on firmer ground, but total awareness is not possible. The effort he makes toward awareness however, deprives him of the very reality he seeks, in that during the time he takes to analyze the reality of what he is and does at a given moment, the moment passes, and he is stifled in it by the inactivity forced on his life by that very reflection. The firmer ground he had sought dissolves into Pascal's "abîme."

In the end, the kind of attitude which leads toward a positive involvement in life is shown in Bernard's progression toward a dynamic acceptance which allows no stagnation, which meets each moment without the prejudice of a fixed and immutable goal. It is both idealistic and realistic at the same time. Bernard's acceptance of life is both a self-realization and a self-transcendence. In a sense Bernard has set out upon a quest, and the Grail he finds is that his rule for life consists in finding all rules within himself: "c'est de trouver cette règle en soi-même; d'avoir pour but le développement de soi" (p. 442). The reality of setting out upon the exciting journey of life is more important than knowing where he is going.

All of the characters are faced with the problem of their attitude toward life, of their identity in relationship to others, to their destiny and to the world, and in the end all of them fail to find an absolute truth to live by. In other words the thematic conclusion of the work lies in the fact that the world and we ourselves cannot be analyzed and explained unless we cease to search for absolutes and simply live òur lives. Living our lives is the only reality. Life is an experiment. Since there are no ready-made formulas we can impose upon existence, existence itself must be our guide. If it is not we face the unavoidable fate of becoming counterfeit.

CHAPTER V

THE SPHINX OF SELF-DELUSION: THEMES OF THE PLOT

When we take a cursory look at the plot structure of *Les Faux-Monnayeurs* we might say that, because on a warm Wednesday afternoon in June a clock happened to be broken in the house of Albéric Profitendieu, a young boy discovers his illegitimacy and runs away. Because he spent his first night away from home with his friend Olivier he learns of Edouard, follows him the next day, gets hold of his suitcase, discovers Edouard's secrets, because of them meets Laura, and travels with both of them to meet Boris whose roommate he will later become in the pension Vedel-Azaïs. Similar cause-effect relationships can be established for the other main characters, and the actions of one always lead to an encounter with another who in turn may lead to an encounter with a third party who may or may not be led to meet the first, but who are all necessary for the overall development of the plot. Thus Vincent, Olivier's brother, becomes our first direct link to Robert de Passavant, who introduces Vincent to Lady Griffith, who influences Vincent to abandon Laura, who then appeals to Edouard for help. In a similar manner Laura, as Edouard's former girl friend serves as pretext to introduce us to Edouard's past which includes the friendship with the members of the Vedel pension and his old piano teacher La Pérouse whom he sees again on the occasion of Laura's wedding and whose grandson offers the pretext for the trip to Saas-Fée.

The various threads of the plot are thus woven together into an intricate fabric which all seem to lead up to Boris's suicide and its consequences. Gide has brought the individual characters out into the arena of life and related them in various and devious ways to each other. Then he drops a bomb in their midst which leaves Boris dead in the center of the arena, while the others scatter and scurry back to the protection of the bleachers. The very fact that it is impossible to exclude even minor characters from sharing a part in the responsibility for Boris's death demonstrates the intricate and conscious composition of the plot on the part of Gide, a fact which alone should prove how essentially coherent the novel is. Gide said in his *Journal des Faux-Monnayeurs*: "Je tâche à enrouler les fils divers de l'intrigue et la complexité de mes pensées autour de ces petites bobines vivantes que sont chacun de mes personnages." [1]

When we penetrate deeper into our characters and leave the purely contingent incident aside we are faced with the intriguing and mysterious workings of the human psyche. An incident combined with a character's predispositions sets the mechanism of motivational forces into action. Various aspects of a character's personality traits and tendencies work together and like cogs on a wheel mesh with the gear of an event in the person's life and generate directional forces. Hence, as Gide states: "Le plus petit geste exige une motivation infinie." [2]

Why does Bernard run away from home and why does he return to it? Why does Edouard not marry Laura, and what makes him incapable of writing his novel? What is it in Olivier which leads him to attempt suicide? Why does Armand Vedel destroy everything he respects most, and why does Laura return to her husband? Why does Monsieur La Pérouse feel duped by life and try to kill himself? And finally, why does Boris actually go through with what was first conceived as an inconsequential childish prank? These are questions which an analysis of the plot will attempt to answer.

We feel from the beginning that Bernard has a tendency to exaggerate, to overplay his rôle, to make drama into melodrama. He is a naturally curious, highly intelligent, generous and perceptive young boy who has spent the better part of his seventeen

---

[1] "Journal des Faux-Monnayeurs," *OC XIII*, p. 14.
[2] *Ibid.*, p. 27.

years sitting in the stuffy classroom. He senses a vague need to get away from it all realizing that life is out there waiting to be lived. "Je sens un immense besoin d'aérer un peu mes pensées" (p. 9), he says. After finding the hidden love letters his decision to leave is apparently as sudden as it is irrevocable. But his uncertainty is betrayed by the note of defiance in the letter written to his father and the fact that he only tells Antoine, the servant, of his departure. The reason for this is stated as follows: "De plus Bernard n'aurait pu leur [aux parents] dire adieu sans qu'ils cherchassent à le retenir. Il redoutait les explications" (p. 20). Why does he fear explanations? May it be that Bernard really does not know why he is leaving and that the discovery of his illegitimacy is merely a welcome pretext for a deep and inexplicable yearning for freedom and adventure?

His formula for action is expressed by his frequent reminder in front of the possibilities of life that it is up to him to act, that no one else but he is faced with the same possibilities. "Si tu ne fais pas cela, qui le fera? Si tu ne le fais pas aussitôt, quand sera-ce" (p. 72)? This immediacy and availability predispose him to certain reactions toward life's situations and become the motivating forces which give the impetus to his deeds, but, because there is no sustaining purpose or goal the initial impulse to action is modified and weakens. His energy without a clearly defined purpose flairs brightly and peters out as a new situation arises to which he reacts quite differently. Thus the habitual response he has cultivated in reacting against the established norms of behavior by rebelling turns against rebellion itself. "L'habitude qu'il a prise de la révolte et de l'opposition le pousse à se révolter contre sa révolte même" (p. 276).

His very attitude of "disponibilité" makes it possible for him to be audacious one moment and conservative the next. Having rudely read Edouard's Journal and taken it on himself to aid Laura he becomes her devoted and loyal servant. "J'aspirais à la liberté comme à un bien suprême, et je n'ai pas plus tôt été libre que je me suis soumis à vous..." (p. 247), he tells Laura. Because of his relationship to Laura he begins to realize that the reasons he has given himself for his actions and attitudes have been wrong. "La route est longue qui mène de ce que je croyais être à ce que peut-être je suis" (p. 245). Realizing this he recognizes that he has wronged his father in accusing him of not loving him, that his reasons for leaving cannot be stated as simply as that. He realizes, then, that he cannot blame others for what had been a mysterious necessity of his being. We frequently find ourselves giving ourselves reasons for the acts we intend to do and afterwards justifications for the acts we have performed which have nothing to do with our real motivations. It is this fact that Bernard now realizes: "Je jouais un affreux personnage, m'efforcais de lui ressembler. Quand je songe à la lettre que j'écrivais à mon faux père avant de quitter la maison, j'ai grand'honte, je vous assure" (p. 247). The desire for absolute freedom which Bernard had conceived as his motivational purpose in life slowly recedes in front of the realization that the total freedom he sought was not only contrary to his true nature, but also made him into something he was not.

Because he sought absolute freedom he had become a slave to his own ideology. This fact leads him to the recognition that to be truly himself, he must find the reasons for his actions within himself. His purpose in life is no longer to *be* free to be what he has predetermined that he should be, but to *become* authentically and genuinely himself. "Je voudrais, tout le long de ma vie, au moindre choc, rendre un son pur, probe, authentique." We may discern in these words the youthful impetuousness of his earlier exclamations, still a trace of melodrama. Yet this desire to be authentic becomes the conscious purpose he gives his life, and his later actions prove that he had indeed been sincere in his desire to be so.

Subconsciously other forces are at work which will lead Bernard away from his conscious purpose. They are curiosity and pride. Ever since Bernard had read Edouard's Journal and realized that there was part of Olivier's life which he had completely ignored his curiosity was aroused concerning the Vedel-Azaïs establishment. After learning of the relationships of Edouard and Laura to the pension he becomes eager to know Armand and Sarah. Therefore when his pride sought to protect him from being rejected by Edouard he hastily conceived the apparently spontaneous idea of moving into the pension on the noble pretext of becoming Boris's companion.

> S'il ne venait pas d'inventer ce beau projet à l'instant même, il en eût déjà parlé à Laura. Mais ce qui était vrai,

> et *qu'il ne se disait pas*, c'est que depuis son indiscrète lecture du journal d'Edouard et depuis la rencontre de Laura, il songeait souvent à la pension Vedel... (p. 272; my italics)

The important detail which Gide inserts is that Bernard was not himself aware of the elements of curiosity and pride which contributed to his apparently spontaneous decision.

By the time we encounter Bernard again he stands at the crossroads of his life, for, though he is still motivated by his desire to be authentic, he himself does not know which direction his "authenticity" will take. He only knows what he does not want to do. In between examination periods he tells Olivier:

> Et puis, mon vieux, si je commence à très bien savoir ce que je ne veux pas faire, je ne sais pas encore bien ce que je ferai. Je ne sais même pas si j'écrirai.... Il me semble parfois qu'écrire empêche de vivre, et qu'on peut s'exprimer mieux par des actes que par des mots. (p. 339)

Indeed, acts will soon follow. Bernard pays only lip service to the nobility to which he lays claim: "depuis que je la [Laura] connais je n'ai plus de désirs du tout.... Je crois que je me méprenais sur moi-même et que ma nature est très chaste" (p. 341), for he spends that very night in Sarah's arms. Granted it is Armand who locks Bernard up in Sarah's room, and Sarah is a more than willing partner, the fact is that Bernard had been sorely mistaken about his own capacity for passion, although he admits to Olivier:

> ...ma turbulence intérieure m'oppresse et j'aspire à la discipliner. C'est comme de la vapeur en moi; elle peut s'échapper en sifflant (ça, c'est la poésie), actionner des pistons, des roues; ou même faire éclater la machine. (p. 342)

Like the romantic hero Hernani, whom Monsieur La Pérouse decries as immoral, Bernard is "une force qui va." At this point his motivations are made up of blind forces which drive but do not direct.

His high esteem for Laura, which he claims is a love which will never cease to grow, seems to be placed in doubt by his capacity to conceive a physical passion for Sarah. And yet that very platonic love for Laura may be the reason for his actions. It is obvious that love plays no part in his relationship to Sarah. Perhaps we must attribute his affair with her again to his youthful curiosity and accept it as part of the natural development of a boy entering manhood. Though his curiosity may be satisfied, he is troubled, and seeks in vain to repress Laura's image which haunts him and keeps him from concentrating on his studies. Rachel's attitude toward him serves to heighten his uneasiness and out of the struggle of his conscience and the recognition of the aimlessness of his previous behavior arises a fresh awareness which motivates him to search for a new meaning to his life, which would preserve his personal integrity and at the same time grant him a purpose beyond authenticity which would place his actions above the mere workings of chance.

At this stage in Bernard's development Gide chooses to emphasize his struggle symbolically by the appearance of an angel to guide him from place to place in order for him to see the world and himself as they really are. The angel, visible only to Bernard, appears at the very moment when he feels at loose ends and very alone. Bernard follows the angel to a church and kneels beside him at the altar. His generous nature prompts him, although he does not believe in God, to feel the urge to self-sacrifice, and the angel reminds him that he offered himself thus to Laura.

Later the angel asks the question which Bernard must ask of himself: "Laisseras-tu disposer de toi le hasard" (p. 434)? After Bernard's plea for guidance the angel shows him various solutions to his search for a goal to his life which Bernard must reject, because he has become aware that no one can give him ready-made what he must find for himself. It took courage for him to assume the responsibility for his personal freedom when he refused to sign up and commit himself to a political or spiritual ideology. Although his conscious motivation in refusing is merely an intuitive disgust with so simple an answer, confirmed by the presence of his older brother in the group, he is at least aware that the sacrifice of self to an immutable goal without regard to the individual nature of that self is absurd, for the nature of man's personality is dynamic and ever-changing. Absolute commitment to an absolute goal therefore becomes impossible to the person who has become aware that he himself is not a fixed and static entity. To preserve his desire to be authentic Bernard must remain free from the limitations that any fixed purpose would impose upon his development. This, however, leaves Bernard faced with the dilemma the angel had pointed out. Without a goal chance will dictate what he is to become. Indeed, there seems to be no alternative to the fact that the chance happenings of life, the chronological sequence of events, will mold the individual, and after a sleepless night of struggle neither the angel nor Bernard emerge victorious from the battle.[3] There seems to be no solution except the one of his immediate intuitive response to a situation which is the gratuitous act.

Bernard's search for a goal, though futile, has changed him. Thus his immediate reaction to Rachel's sorrow is to leave the pension matured by the realization that though he is free to act, his freedom of action may be harmful to others as well as to himself. That is why Edouard's proposed solution of finding his rule of conduct within himself arouses Bernard's apprehensive reflection: "Si encore j'étais certain de préférer en moi le meilleur... mais je ne parviens pas même à connaître ce que j'ai de meilleur en moi..." (p. 442). The question of the moral nature of our acts, whether they be qualified as good or evil, must remain open, because, if we cannot be sincere by living according to absolute standards, then we cannot predetermine what is good and what is evil. Our actions must be a response to concrete situations and what may be good in one situation may be evil in another. Therefore Edouard's counsel which may appear deceptively simple is the only answer to an extremely difficult existential problem: "Vous ne pouvez... apprendre comment vivre, qu'en vivant" (p. 443). And even if, as Bernard wonders, he lives badly that of itself will be a constructive lesson for the future. In the end the practical motivational basis for Bernard's life achieves its fullest expression in the only formula Bernard and Edouard can accept: "Il est bon de suivre sa pente, pourvu que ce soit en montant" (p. 443).

In the themes of the story we have observed Bernard's' progression from absolute moral freedom to a sense of moral respon-

---

[3] It is interesting to compare this episode with the biblical account of Jacob's struggle with the angel. Jacob emerges victorious and receives a new identity. From now on, the angel tells him, he shall be known as Israel.

sibility for what he is to become in relationship to others as well as to himself. In the plot this sense of moral responsibility is expressed by his changed motivations from a vague yearning to be free to be himself, to the desire to accept that freedom only as long as it is an authentic response to a concrete situation and at the same time not harmful to others. His purpose of being at all times true to himself remains his valid goal in life. His adventures, however, have taught him that being true to himself means to accept the fact that the only authentic "self" that man can have is the one that he himself creates "en suivant sa pente."

Edouard moves on two different levels in the novel, the one on which he is a human being and the one on which he is a professional artist. The two seldom coincide which makes for Edouard's elusiveness and basic lack of unity. This also accounts for the fact that he is almost impossible to analyze. We cannot trust his Journal when he speaks about himself, because he so often deludes himself. Yet he is basically a kind person who deplores the mores of society which force people into preconceived molds and make them into something they are not. He has a disarming openness and lack of prejudice about him which make him be amused rather than disturbed when he encounters various aberrations of behavior; indeed, he encourages them in the course of the novel and then declines all responsibility for the consequences.

Many factors contribute to his attitude, and one of the main motivations which drives him to such meddling curiosity is his hatred and abhorrence of all influences which stifle and suppress the creative forces in man. Having himself escaped from the atrophying influences of a puritanical upbringing and education he cannot stand idly by while others cut off their creative potential by accepting to live in a world of preestablished norms of behavior. He accepts Bernard as his secretary, even though he has stolen his suitcase, because he is entertained and amused by the possibilities this relationship may offer him. Edouard even recognizes the danger in this attitude: "Le danger c'est que je prends à tout événement inattendu un amusement si vif qu'il me fait perdre de vue le but à atteindre." (p. 198)

Edouard is incapable of lasting relationships. His doubts concerning the reality of his emotions toward the other person, the need to analyze everything that happens to him, make him lack stability. He senses that he is incapable of sustaining one emotion very long, that he must exert a constant effort to do so and that as soon as he realizes that he is making the effort, the emotion is weakened by that very recognition. He is even disarmingly honest about this tendency of his nature and the very fact that he so readily explains it may serve to obscure the real reasons behind his actions of which he himself is not conscious. It is in any case a marvelous excuse and cover-up for his shortcomings and the only real reason he gives for not marrying Laura: "Un tel être n'est pas de ceux qu'on épouse. Comment faire comprendre cela à Laura" (p. 90)?

Behind Edouard's lack of stability and consistency a sadistic streak is discernable, for the very amusement and entertainment he derives from moving the people he encounters around on the chess board of life (even though he says it is for artistic reasons) is a trait of diabolical sadism which is all the more perplexing, since he does not feel any twinge of conscience after his chess pieces end up in checkmate. After rereading Laura's letter in the train which tells of her plight he merely shrugs his shoulders. He is willing to help her out, but becomes more interested in Boris and Bernard in the process. After Boris's death he claims that he will not be able to use the incident in his novel, because it lacked sufficient motivation. In other words Edouard is incapable of recognizing his own share of guilt in what has happened to Laura and Boris. The rationalizations of his motives — he thinks of himself as generous and allowing others complete freedom of action — is very much akin to the blindness he so vigorously deplores in others. He is thus practicing the worst form of self-delusion.

His professed purpose is to write a novel on the subject of *Les Faux-Monnayeurs* and since he conceives of this novel as something never before attempted where he, as an artist, must have complete freedom of action in order to be creative, he subordinates human values to the artistic goal. Only when the two elements coincide can he succeed in being human and achieve artistically. Essentially this is what happens in his relationship with Olivier and significantly it is only while nursing Olivier back to health, whom he genuinely loves, that he is able to write several chapters of his novel. Edouard needs another person in whom to find a reflection of himself and a sense of his own reality, and yet the other person must leave him free to be creative. This is why the homosexual relationship becomes more desirable to him than the idea of marriage which would be too binding.

That which saves Edouard from being disliked and which endears him to the other characters in the novel is his genuine interest in other people of all walks of life and his willingness to listen. Others typically seek no other reason for his interest than his innate goodness, all the more so, since they are extremely flattered by his attention. His interest in Monsieur La Pérouse and the financial health of the pension is motivated by genuine concern mixed with the feeling of his own importance as the person whom others can call on in times of trouble. Yet even behind his concern for Georges who is on the verge of getting into real trouble, if apprehended by the police, lies his unquenchable curiosity about Georges' reaction to a similar incident in the novel he is writing.

> Chaque être agit selon sa loi, et celle d'Edouard le porte à expérimenter sans cesse. Il a bon coeur assurément, mais souvent je préférerais, pour le repos d'autrui, le voir agir par intérêt; car la générosité qui l'entraîne n'est souvent que la compagne d'une curiosité qui pourrait devenir cruelle. (p. 274)

As long as his manoeuvering of other peoples' lives serves the purpose of his art he feels it is justifiable. This renders his reaction to Boris's death all the more condemnable.

When the author stops to analyze his characters he asks a most revealing question about Edouard:

> Ce qui ne me plaît pas chez Edouard ce sont les raisons qu'il se donne. Pourquoi cherche-t-il à se persuader, à présent, qu'il conspire au bien de Boris? Mentir aux autres, passe encore; mais à soi-même! Le torrent qui noie un enfant prétend-il lui porter à boire?... (p. 275)

His real motive is the cruel curiosity of a creator who wants to place his characters into explosive situations to observe how they burn and who does not even feel responsible for the ashes. Essentially what keeps Edouard from even recognizing his own responsibility is his inability to face reality and accept it. Edouard's rationalizations over his reasons for leaving Boris's death out of his book is the unquestionable proof of his not being able to cope with reality and therefore to accept his share of guilt.

Behind his evasion of reality lies a lurking fear of coming face to face with the true reflection of his motives. He prefers to think that Boris's motives were insufficient and inexplicable, he even calls them indecent. Edouard had certainly not foreseen the terrible consequences of his actions which at first appeared to be motivated only by the purely altruistic desire to give Monsieur La Pérouse the pleasure of knowing his grandson. Indeed, we may surmise that his desire to please his old piano teacher was so great that his ability to face the truth about Boris's needs was impaired. Yet in the light of what Edouard has already revealed about the pension, the hope he expresses about Boris's potential in such an atmosphere smacks of lugubrious hypocrisy. "Je compte beaucoup sur l'atmosphère de la pension Azaïs et de Paris pour faire de Boris un travailleur; pour le guérir enfin de la recherche des 'biens imaginaires.' C'est là pour lui, qu'est le salut" (p. 263). Surely he cannot really believe that this young impressionable boy who is essentially pure would flourish in an atmosphere where Edouard had earlier remarked that flowers even seemed out of place, as though they should wither before his very eyes.

In the themes of the story we have found that Edouard tries to base his attitude toward life on total awareness and, that because total awareness is impossible, he fails trapped in the futility of his effort. The plot has revealed that the conscious motivation behind his actions is his desire for complete honesty with himself and with life and his abhorrence of all traces of hypocrisy and blindness in others. Ironically, however, his subconscious fears keep him from facing a reality which may condemn his artistic freedom and resulting lack of responsibility. He stands thus severely judged by the very criteria whereby he judges others. Gide's severity toward Edouard is too evident, too subtly drawn, to be an accident of artistic creation. Gide is hereby condemning the artist who places his "rôle d'inquiéteur" beyond the reach of social and human responsibility.

Olivier longs to communicate his real emotions, but is not only afraid of not being able to but also of being rejected if he were to do so. His very desire for close friendship keeps him at a distance from those he loves most. When he receives Bernard's letter about his experiences in Saas-Fée with Laura and Edouard Olivier cannot rationally control his emotions of despair which, because he loves Edouard and is jealous of Bernard's imagined relationship with him, turns into spite and the desire on his part to hurt the one who has hurt him. The way to Olivier's unfortunate departure had been carefully prepared by Passavant's machinations, his flattering offer of the editorship of a review, and his engagement of a supporting force in Vincent whose own rationalizations of his motives had made him Passavant's ally in persuading the Molinier family to let Olivier go off with him. The letter was only the straw that broke the camel's back, which brought the mixture of contrary emotions together in an uncontrollable rage and despair. "Cette nuit, les démons de l'enfer l'habitèrent. Le lendemain matin il se précipita chez Robert. Le comte de Passavant l'attendait" (p. 215).

In his subsequent letter to Bernard he claims that it was Bernard's letter which gave him the courage to act, but when he speaks about his surprise that Vincent should have helped him to his departure he seems to be pleading his own case rather than Vincent's:

> Nous avons, à notre âge, une fâcheuse tendance à juger les gens trop sévèrement et à condamner sans appel. Bien des actes nous apparaissent répréhensibles, odieux même, simplement parce que nous n'en pénétrons pas suffisamment les motifs. (pp. 264-265)

The only sincere words in the letter were the ones he crossed out where he reprimands Edouard for having abandoned him. He obviously crossed them out, because, consciously or unconsciously, he wanted to hurt Edouard by not mentioning him. His vulnerability lies in his very fear of being hurt which is in part the reason behind his attempted suicide after his night with Edouard. Montaigne said: "Qui craint de souffrir, il souffre desja de ce qu'il craint." Having achieved what was to him the supreme moment of acceptance and joy he is afraid of the pain which will result from the fact that it may not happen again. The impulse which drove him to open the gas knob in Edouard's bathroom is more complex than Olivier realized. It may have had no conscious purpose at all and have been motivated by Olivier's need to communicate by means of a drastic act precisely that which he could not put into words, while a possible hope of being revived in extremis made him choose gas-poisoning rather than some quicker method of death, in which case he may have subconsciously calculated that it would be normal for Edouard to nurse him back to health and he would have a natural excuse to be close to him for quite some time.

There is no simple answer as to why Olivier sought to kill himself. Reasons, conscious desires, and subconscious fears are intricately intertwined. The image of spinning faces in the unreal atmosphere of the Argonaut banquet, Jarry's absurd threat to "tuder" Lucien Bercail, the vision of intimacy between Sarah and Bernard, his own vague ostentatious threats to Dhurmer and his echoing refrain "pas touché... pas touché," his blinding tears of humiliation in front of Edouard, the weight of a whole summer wasted with Passavant, the silent reproach in Bernard's eyes, the touch of Edouard's protective hand, the significance of the "tutoiement," and finally, their reconciliation and night together all emerge simultaneously in an explosive moment which gives birth to the impulse to self-destruction and makes Olivier a realistic human being of flesh and blood. His suicide attempt can be considered what Gide defines as the gratuitous act. Gide explains:

> Je ne crois pas du tout moi-même, à l'acte gratuit, c'est-à-dire à un acte qui ne serait motivé par rien. Cela est essentiellement inadmissible.... Les mots "acte gratuit" sont une étiquette *provisoire* qui m'a paru commode pour désigner les actes qui échappent aux explications psychologiques ordinaires, les gestes que ne détermine pas le simple intérêt personnel... [4]

Laura's love for Edouard causes her to appeal to him for help with the secret hope that he would not only come to her rescue but would again become involved with her. It was her love for Edouard which caused her to marry Douviers on the rebound and "dans les bras de Vincent, c'était Edouard encore qu'elle

---

[4] "Faits-divers," *La Nouvelle Revue Française*, June 1928, p. 841.

cherchait." When he remains aloof she begins to seek the reasons in herself and pathetically depreciates her own worth and reason for being. Bernard's devotion saves her from complete self-depreciation and from disgust and perhaps indirectly reminds her of Douviers, her husband, who is just as devoted to her and has the legal right to be so. Realizing in Saas-Fée that what Edouard had done to her she was in the process of doing to her husband, she recognizes that even if she herself cannot attain happiness, it may be in her power to make her husband happy. Faced with the inalterable fact that Edouard no longer loves her she accepts the inevitable and confesses to her husband, who forgives her graciously. Acceptance of mediocre happiness and emotional security become preferable to the emotional upheaval in which she had lived in trying to find Edouard in every man she met. Her motivations have changed from her both conscious and unconscious search for the Edouard she loved, but who no longer exists, to a resigned willingness to trade her dream of a passionate love for the reality of the affectionate loyalty of her husband.

The fact that she is not capable of feigning a love for Douviers which she does not feel drives him to a precipitous journey to see Edouard whose contrition and tears he obviously misinterprets. Too naïve to recognize that others are not always what they seem to be he lacks the imagination to appear other than he actually is. Although he claims to be the jealous rival and sets out with that intention, he cannot go through with it and consciously assume a rôle which is not his. He thus represents along with Bernard the only other person in the novel who cannot be called counterfeit.

Bernard cannot be called a counterfeit personality because his development has led him to refuse to subject his actions to a concept of a preestablished and fixed identity. Douviers cannot be called a counterfeit personality, since he never becomes aware of a dichotomy between function and identity, between what he is and who he is. Edouard accuses him of lack of imagination. His outlook may also be attributed to a state of innocence where life has not yet offered him of the tree of knowledge, where motivations and purposes are one and the same, and where all his acts fit into explicable patterns. Unfortunately his very state of innocence deprives him of a human dimension. For opposite reasons the same dimension is lacking in the sophisticated and evil Lilian Griffith, and Vincent similarly loses his human attributes in the end. When the soul of man is no longer the battle field between good and evil, he loses the very qualities which make him human. Vincent, as he is revealed at the close of the novel by Alexandre's letter, believes he has become the devil incarnate. Absolute identification with evil is as unproductive as complete though blissful unawareness of it. It is forever the middle ground to which most mortals are condemned that will be the true subject of the novelist.

The stages through which Vincent passes are so explicitly drawn in the novel that a summary of his motivations will suffice. Vanity and greed are the two character traits which lead to his downfall. The rationalizations which accompany his acts are derived from his complete lack of a belief in the supernatural and therefore his denial of the existence of an evil power. All the more vulnerable to temptation he can no longer act without sublimating the reasons for his actions. Dependent on reason and the rational process his mind slowly disintegrates, and everything that does not fit into his scheme drives him to madness. Any system which would seek to give rational explanations for all our acts breaks down on the very fallacy that such explanations are feasible, even possible. He is a scientist, and the fact that the inner depth of the psychic life cannot be measured by the quantitative methods of science drives him insane. Significantly he denies the possibility of the demonic until faced with the ineluctable evidence of his life: He has murdered Lilian. He then becomes convinced that he himself is the devil. Since he had denied the possibility of an evil power outside himself, he must conclude that he himself must be the source of evil.

By birth endowed with means and the impressive title of comte, Robert de Passavant has written the script for his rôle in life and given himself the starring part. His purpose is to impress and to please. But behind Passavant's façade there is a gnawing fear of inadequacy, inadequacy as a person and as an artist. His elegance, his amiable manner, his condescending behavior are all part of the mask which conceal a frightening feeling of inferiority. His part includes the affectation of superiority with the theatrical props of expensive cigarettes and port accompanied by the hollow social banter of flippant and inane conversation which he has rehearsed so well that, once we know its pattern, we discern that it repeats itself almost verbatim throughout the book. Even his gestures seem to have been studied for their effect. The reason behind his creation of a literary review lies in his desire to manipulate behind the scenes and to insert anonymous eulogies of his own work. The reason for appointing Olivier to be editor is not because of his literary abilities which are doubtful, but lies in Olivier's childlike admiration and the personal build-up Passavant derives from his innocent adulation. The reason for his debauching trip with Olivier to Corsica lies not only in his homosexual tendencies, but also in the fact that he finds in Olivier an ego-building mirror in which to admire his reflection. "Habile à séduire et habitué à plaire, Passavant avait besoin de sentir en face de lui un miroir complaisant pour briller" (p. 368).

Passavant is so afraid of doing something out of character that he lacks character altogether. When his father dies he reacts with indifference, not so much because he wants to hide any genuine emotion he might have, but because of the theatrical effect his calm little sentence in the midst of pleasantries hopes to achieve: "Ah! j'oubliais de vous dire: il est mort..." His explanation for his indifference is ironically the following: "J'ai horreur des sentiments tout faits" (p. 54). When Olivier finally escapes from his hold over him he accepts it as good riddance, not even daring to let on to himself that he might be affected by the loss:

> Pour n'avoir pas à reconnaître ses défaites, il affectait toujours d'avoir souhaité son sort, et quoi qu'il advînt, il prétendait l'avoir voulu. (p. 405)

His is an attitude of a person who is afraid to be hurt by life and has cushioned himself in so many layers of false indifference against the shocks of reality that the authentic core is forever lost. Pathetically, his theatrical presentation fools no one more than himself.

In the story we have seen that Passavant consistently plays a rôle. The plot has shown us why. Passavant is driven by a relentless fear of being weighed and found wanting: he therefore assumes a counterfeit rôle in society hoping that the addition of the costume will weigh the scale down in his favor.

Armand Vedel half seriously and half jokingly describes his problems in his "traité d'insuffisance". The tragedy of his life lies in his inadequacy, but contrary to Passavant he does not seek to cover it up, but accentuates it to the point of despair. "Je n'ai le sentiment que de mes manques. Manque d'argent, manque de forces, manque d'esprit, manque d'amour" (p. 359). In his cynicism that which he mentions last is most likely that which he feels the most — his "manque d'amour". He is crying out for love in the only way he knows how, and no one in his family knows how to listen. Underneath his sarcastic self-depreciation lies a desperate yearning for tenderness and affection. His apparent lack of sensitivity comes from his intense susceptibility. He laughs in order not to cry. He hardens himself against life, in order to conceal his vulnerability. He destroys that which he respects and loves most. His masochistic tendencies afford him a perverse pleasure in his own misery.

In a way of life in which he is aware enough to know that there is no meaning and insufficient to provide one what possible purpose can Armand give to existence? Rather than asking the questions we must ask about Olivier and Boris, namely what motivates their suicide, here we are faced with the opposite question: What keeps Armand Vedel alive? In an absurd world where he has denied the values given by preceding generations, where life takes on a meaninglessness which expresses itself in the dark, seamy, and destitute identity he finds in comparing himself to a "vase nocturne," what unconscious hope sustains his life? "C'est une arête étroite, sur laquelle mon esprit se promène, cette ligne de démarcation entre l'être et le non-être" (p. 360). It is significant that the real model for the character of Armand, Armand Bavratel, whom Gide describes in *Si le grain ne meurt* actually committed suicide. Armand does not kill himself, at least not conventionally, but refusing to see a doctor and to be treated for a curable but otherwise fatal disease amounts to almost the same thing, and significantly, his death will eventually be brought about by the very insufficiency which characterized his life.

Rachel is the only person whom he respects, and he deliberately makes her suffer. He claims he makes her suffer because of his abomination of virtue:

> Je crois que c'est ce que j'ai de plus sincère en moi:
> l'horreur, la haine de tout ce qu'on appelle Vertu. Ne
> cherche pas à comprendre. Tu ne sais pas ce que peut
> faire de nous une première éducation puritaine. Elle
> vous laisse au coeur un ressentiment dont on ne peut plus
> jamais se guérir... (p. 469)

And yet he loves her precisely because she is virtuous. This unusual contradiction in his nature gives him opposing impulses which, aroused simultaneously, seem to exhaust each other on the other's extreme.

Armand's warped outlook on life stems from his puritanical background and his unsatisfied yearning for attention. When he depreciates himself to the point of calling himself a receptacle for human excrement he is subconsciously challenging life to give him a meaning beyond the ridiculous blindness of his family and an answer to the insoluble problem of the existence of evil and suffering. Unable to find meaning in a faith which has given him only sorry examples of humanity he finds nothing to give a purpose or goal to his life. Rarely does he seem motivated by more than a destructive response toward life which has almost become habitual.

In the themes of the story we described Armand's rejection of life as a blindness which doubts the existence of any answers to existence. In the themes of the plot we find that a desperate and unsuccessful search to find affection and meaning in life dwindles to an almost total lack of purpose where actions are not the result of a conscious motivation, but where the daily course of events elicits only life-weary and for the most part destructive responses.

The examination of Boris's personality, motivations, and purposes is one of the most complex in the novel, and his suicide constitutes a climatic explosion which shakes the very foundation of the other characters' beliefs. Boris is a neurotic and already under psychiatric care when we encounter him in Saas-Fée. The very first sentence Edouard overhears demonstrates the anxious ambivalence of his personality: "Oui, je veux bien. Non, je ne veux pas" (p. 217). Madame Sophroniska analyzes him in great detail and from her observations we can determine some of the reasons for his malady, but contrary to her overconfident convictions we cannot claim to understand each mysterious particle of his tormented psyche. Boris is just a child, and in the course of his thirteen years he has had the misfortune of being born into a home where he had no legal father and where his mother, though at times overprotective, dragged him into the cheaper entertainment circles of Warsaw where she had to make a living. Introduced to clandestine activity by his schoolmate Baptistin Kraft, who called their actions a magical initiation into the superior realm of illimited power believing that the use of their secret formula had the power to fill the void of their lives with imaginary ecstasy, Boris soon succumbed to the voluptuous escape he found in the practice. Confronted by his mother's violent disapproval and the subsequent death of his father the habit took on the proportion of a deadly sin, which led to his neurotic conviction that he was directly responsible for his father's death. The belief in his own unworthiness and guilt reinforced by the moral nature of his upbringing convinced him that he was obsessed by the devil and unclean, that he would never be able to see an angel or associate with purity, and that the result of his sin was the eternal perdition of his soul.

Madame Sophroniska's efforts with Boris are limited to her penetration into these dark secrets, her nonchalant acceptance of their naturalness, and her subsequent attempt to convince Boris that he is a normal little boy. Edouard senses the inadequacy of the method. He recognizes that the outward signs of neurosis have disappeared but reflects:

> ...il me semble que la maladie s'est simplement réfugiée dans une région plus profonde de l'être, comme pour échapper au regard inquisiteur du médecin; et que c'est à présent l'âme même qui est atteinte. (p. 261)

> De même qu'à l'onanisme avaient succédé les mouvements nerveux, ceux-ci cèdent à présent à je ne sais quelle transe invisible! (p. 262)

Bronja is the only person he can communicate with, because she accepts him naïvely on his own terms. But even she is frightened by his insistence on his need for purification, his obsession of wiping off everything he touches before handing it to her, and his spontaneous urge to cleanse himself naked in the snow.

After his arrival at the Vedel pension his shyness, emotivity, and obvious anxiety are natural targets for the older boys who have made cruelty a defiant mode of assertion of their imagined superiority. Deeply perplexed by his own exclusion and completely obsessed by his desire to belong, he is flattered by Georges' sudden attention, even though he suspects foul play. In his innocence and need to give of himself he is motivated by a deep yearning to belong to the human race no matter what the cost. After Bronja's death one last link to his fellowman is gone, the world has become a desert:

> Le monde entier lui paraissait désert. Sa mère était trop loin de lui, toujours absente; son grand-père, trop vieux; même Bernard n'était plus là, près duquel il prenait confiance... Une âme tendre comme la sienne a besoin de quelqu'un vers qui porter en offrande sa noblesse et sa pureté. Il n'avait pas assez d'orgueil pour s'y complaire. Il avait aimé Bronja beaucoup trop pour pouvoir espérer retrouver jamais cette raison d'aimer qu'il perdait avec elle. Les anges qu'il souhaitait de voir, désormais, sans elle, comment y croire? Même son ciel à présent se vidait.
> (p. 475)

Combined now with his intense yearning to belong is his quiet desperation of ever having the chance to prove himself.

Suddenly the occasion offers itself. The diabolical plan has been conceived; the talisman has been cleverly planted on his desk which is enough to send him back to his former obsession; Georges has made the proper overtures to friendship. Boris becomes a victim of powers beyond his control and comprehension. He is already emotionally disturbed and unbelievably lonesome when these incomprehensible forces bring back all the guilt feelings that he had repressed in connection with his masturbation. The apparently supernatural appearance of his forgotten talisman conjures up his old belief that he is impure and condemned to eternal perdition. Motivated by his anguished sense of guilt, his need for acceptance, his fatal conviction that all is lost in any case, he accepts the challenge of the "confrérie des hommes forts" vaguely realizing that he is being played for a sucker. Out of the depths of his despair is born the need for self-assertion even if it should result in self-destruction, as he now realizes it must. He complies with the rules of the *confrérie*. His intention of going through with the plan becomes absolute and irrevocable. Once this goal is envisioned all else falls into oblivion. Boris perceives only the chalked circle in the corner and the weight of the gun in his pocket. He responds to all stimuli as a robot or sleepwalker, as a person in a trance to whom reality no longer exists and only the goal to reach — the circle and the gun — stand out in his consciousness. He vaguely tries to pray, but after failing to communicate with his fellowman, he cannot possibly communicate with a Being in whom he does not really believe, but to whom he irrationally attributes the power of eternal judgment. In the end his suicide may in part be motivated by a senseless need for atonement, as it becomes a drastic way to show that he is paying the supreme price for his sin. Still convinced that he was the cause of his father's death he will have given his life in expiation. No god could ask for more. We sense in the desperation of his act an instinctive impulse to placate the gods with human sacrifice, an anxious need as old as the human race.

In the story we found that all the characters are faced with the choice of their attitude toward life and that Boris's final rejection of life itself was simply another manifestation of his rejection of reality in general. In the plot we are confronted with the complexity of man's motivational behavior in the face of extreme emotional conflict and tension. Conflicting motives are at the very core of Boris's personality which exert such urgent pressures on his system that his consciousness can no longer cope with reality. Motivated by his deep need to belong to society and by his estrangement from it, his distorted view of his guilt and his desire to escape from that guilt, faced with the incomprehensible environment of wilful and malicious ostracism his suicide paradoxically becomes the only means he sees to identify with the group. A psychiatrist would call him schizophrenic. Gide simply illustrates Boris's complexity and leaves some of the mystery of his motivational drives intact. Madame Sophroniska's failure to penetrate the secrets of the human soul can be seen as a conscious critique of the limitations of conventional psychiatry and of psychological analysis in the conventional novel.

Finally, from youth's inability to adjust to life we turn to old age and the equally enigmatic character of Boris's grandfather, Monsieur La Pérouse. Whereas Boris responds to life's vicissitudes by rejecting any possibility of a future, La Pérouse looks back on life out of the perspective of old age and recognizes the insignificance of his past. His acts did not have the meaning he attributed to them at the time:

> Oui, je commence seulement à comprendre qu'ils n'ont pas du tout la signification que je croyais jadis en les faisant. C'est maintenant seulement que je comprends que toute ma vie j'ai été dupe. (p. 149)

With old age has come the recognition that underlying his conscious motivations and purposes other forces were at work which stimulated and sustained his actions. Whereas he had thought that he was acting out of a consciously perceived purpose he now reaches the conclusion that he never made a free choice in his life, that life imposed itself upon him, that his freedom of action was an illusion, that man in general labors under the illusion of choosing his own destiny, when, in reality, a malevolent force plays with man like a puppeteer with his puppets.

Edouard is perceptive in analyzing the tragedy behind La Pérouse's life. He compares the loss of man's essence to the Scripture passage: "Si le sel perd sa saveur, avec quoi la lui rendra-t-on?" When man loses the very essence of his being his life becomes meaningless existence. This is the tragedy behind La Pérouse's recognition that he has been living a lie. That which he had thought to be his own decisions and purposes, the very essence of his humanity, turns out to be self-deception. La Pérouse has played the tragic rôle of modern man who has lost his identity and for whom it is too late to create one. Faced with the sudden vapid vision of the meaninglessness of his life La Pérouse resolves to kill himself. One last feeble need binds him to the living, the desire to see his grandson before he dies. Since fate, in the guise of Edouard, brings about this last wish he accepts it as a sign to carry out his intention. He soon finds that he cannot. As he had exhausted the emotion he was to feel at the sight of Boris before he ever met him, likewise he has exhausted his ability to go through with his suicide by the very anticipation of the act. Initially, he ascribes his failure to a lack of courage and his fear of the explosion so close to his ear. But the fear of noise is really only a pretext for a deeper fear of life itself. Death would seem therefore doubly welcome, and yet, pathetically, La Pérouse has ceased to live from the moment he realized that he was not free. In the end this is how he explains his inability to shoot himself. He was not free to do so.

When Edouard visits La Pérouse after Boris's suicide he is greeted by a deceptive calm. La Pérouse never refers to the event, nor does Edouard. Their very silence demonstrates that neither can cope with the incredible reality of Boris's death in particular and of man's death in general. The intricate interplay of human responsibility behind Boris's death is too complicated, too incredible to grasp. La Pérouse seeks a scapegoat, but when no single person is to blame, he lashes out at the cruelty of God.

Pitiful, pathetic, and so very human La Pérouse has seen all his traditional values crumble and unable to cope with the void, he longs for peace and total harmony. Life cannot offer it to him. Since he cannot kill himself he resigns himself to a vegetable-like existence, to a purposelessness which consists of an aimless waiting for the final curtain to fall on the comedy of his life and which is characterized by his habitual responses to his instinctive needs of survival.

In the course of the plot we have seen that the "pure" motive does not exist. The narrator says of Edouard: "...derrière le plus beau motif, souvent se cache un diable habile et qui sait tirer gain de ce qu'on croyait lui ravir" (p. 275).

Good intentions fail; in fact a popular adage has it that the road to hell is paved with them. Love motivates actions but cannot sustain lasting relationships which fall into a disillusioning "décristallisation". Hope more often than not turns to despair, and the benefits of reason are limited to the recognition of the inevitable ignorance of the real consequences of our acts. Indeed, if man cannot even with the best of motivations control the outcome of his acts, can he be held responsible for them? If man cannot be held responsible, then who can? Faced with this awesome question man seeks his scapegoat and lashes out at the Unknown attributing his plight to the workings of the Devil or to the cruelty of God. Why does God remain silent? La Pérouse asks. In the face of human suffering the age-old mystery of God's silence wrenches anguish from his breast to the point that he sets himself up as the judge of God.

La Pérouse concludes: "Dieu s'amuse avec nous comme un chat avec la souris qu'il tourmente." His silence is in reality connivance with the Devil. La Pérouse would therefore ascribe his own ennui to God and attribute creation to a need for entertainment. La Pérouse's reasoning about God's motivations is thus correlative with our conclusions about Edouard's motives, and in a sense, Edouard, the creator of his own microcosm, could be seen as a projection of the Creator of the macrocosm. La Pérouse's judgment of God's motivations is based on his erroneous assumption that we can ascribe human emotions to God. The fact that man invariably does is the atheist's strongest argument for God's non-existence. Man has often created God in order to have someone beyond himself to be responsible for it all. This is why La Pérouse paradoxically affirms he does not believe in God, while in the same breath he blames Him for his plight.

La Pérouse's plight is at the same time the tragic of the too late and the tragic of increased awareness. Had he not become aware he would have continued to live in blissful ignorance. Had he realized earlier that he was living a lie he may have had the opportunity to change. But for him it is too late. For Bernard it was not. The main difference between the two lies not in the number of years, but in their attitude toward freedom. Bernard assumes his freedom and its concomitant responsibility. La Pérouse denies that human freedom exists. Like all other values by which he lived, it was merely another illusion. La Pérouse's attitude would be unacceptable to Bernard who has learned the fallacy behind absolutes. In the absence of absolutes man must assume his own freedom which means at the same time that he must assume the responsibility for his acts. La Pérouse's negative outlook, his belief in the absolute slavery of man, hinders any further evolution of his being.

In the story we have seen that La Pérouse's resignation to the lack of human freedom is an admission of absurd meaninglessness. In the plot we have seen that the assumption of a fixed identity can only be sustained when accompanied by blindness. Once man becomes aware of the insignificant rôle his lofty intentions and most altruistic motives have played in the course of human events, he comes face to face with the absurdity of maintaining any motives inspired by his own fallacious ideals. Reduced to a submission to his own lack of freedom La Pérouse has resigned himself to a life without purpose.

One of the central themes of the plot is the discrepancy between the real motivations of the characters and their own reasons for their actions. We have consistently found that the characters tend to rationalize their motivations, that they very seldom see themselves as they really are and that they therefore misinterpret their motives by either ascribing to them more nobility than they have (Edouard, Olivier, Passavant, Vincent), or by seeing behind their actions more evil than they could possibly lay claim to. (Armand, Boris). The plot exemplifies beautifully the universal truth that man is just as inventive in finding ways to fool himself as he is in any other realm of human endeavor.

Finally, the thematic conclusion of the plot demonstrates that there is not always an *answer* to our questions of 'why?' that most often our motivations are so complex, so subtly intertwined between the conscious awareness of the reasons we give ourselves and the subconscious motivations whose existence we either ignore or repress that it becomes impossible to place our finger on one salient *reason* which makes us act or react in a specific way. In this respect the novel is more realistic than the traditional novel in that it shows the life-like multiplicity of the irrational forces which, derived from our environmental and hereditary backgrounds, make up the inexplicable course of our lives.

If the characters in the novel cannot be explicitly analyzed we must conclude that beyond the purely contingent incident the "plot", as a literary structure which is based on the necessity of one incident generating the next, cannot suffice to explain the deeper coherence of the novel. For that we must turn to an analysis which is based on the affinity of themes by contrast or similarity independent of their linear or causal relationships.

Chapter VI

LUX ET VERITAS:
GENERIC COHERENCE OF THEMES

In the analysis of the themes of the story and the themes of the plot we have observed analogies and interrelationships, but, because of their treatment side by side, the emphasis on incidents and character relationships in the former and on motivational forces in the latter, our picture of the over-all unity of the novel is incomplete. Like a three-dimensional photograph seen without the special colored lenses which come with it, we have discerned only the parallel lines which constitute on the one hand the story and on the other hand the plot. We must now put on those special glasses and bring the entire novel into focus in order to see its depth, a process achieved by relating themes which are generically coherent.

The underlying theme of the entire novel is the problem of reality — its perception, rejection, and distortion. We shall explore the implications of man's struggle to find values by which to live, his conscious and unconscious blindness, his search for universality in the particular representation of reality, the conflict between convention and the individual, the temporal and spatial relativism of man's existence, and the nature of man's essence in a world suffused by darkness and uncertainty.

The Problem of Reality

Beyond the fact that Edouard's Journal is his source book for a novel of the same title there is a clear correlation between Edouard's Journal and the rest of the novel. Edouard theorizes on many aspects of the unfolding incidents of the novel and his general comments often apply to particular incidents of which Edouard has no knowledge. His remarks about "décristallisation" for instance are applied to his own experience with Laura and represent a project for a future novel, but they can be applied to several other incidents as well.

Edouard describes "décristallisation" thus:

> On parle sans cesse de la brusque cristallisation de l'amour. La lente *décristallisation*, dont je n'entends jamais parler, est un phénomène psychologique qui m'intéresse bien davantage.... Quel admirable sujet de roman: au bout de quinze ans, de vingt ans de vie conjugale, la décristallisation progressive et réciproque des conjoints! (p. 91; italics Gide's)

We have already observed the floundering marriage of the Profitendieu couple; this theme will be repeated with the La Pérouse and Molinier couples. A contrasting theme of nascent and developing love is portrayed in the rapid "cristallisation" of Bernard's love for Laura.

The motif of "décristallisation" as introduced by Edouard carries the theme of his observation that the difference between what we feel and what we imagine we feel is imperceptible, that reality and imagined reality are subjectively fused:

> Dans le domaine des sentiments, le réel ne se distingue pas de l'imaginaire. Et s'il suffit d'imaginer qu'on aime pour aimer, ainsi suffit-il de se dire qu'on imagine aimer, quand on aime, pour aussitôt aimer un peu moins, et même pour en détacher quelques cristaux.... (pp. 90-91)

The complex problem of distinguishing between objective and subjective reality is the central theme of the novel as Edouard states elsewhere repeatedly when discussing the theory of the novel.

Edouard describes his artistic endeavor as the conflict between reality and the novelist's attempt to grasp it. The passages in italics represent linking phrases:

> Ce que je veux, c'est présenter *d'une part la réalité, présenter d'autre part cet effort pour la styliser...* (p. 233)

And:

> J'invente un personnage de romancier, que je pose en figure centrale; et le sujet du livre, si vous voulez, c'est précisément *la lutte entre ce que lui offre la réalité et ce que, lui, prétend en faire.* (p. 233)
>
> A vrai dire, ce sera là le sujet: *la lutte entre les faits proposés par la réalité, et la réalité idéale.* (p. 234)

Still later Edouard returns to this subject in his Journal:

> Je commence à entrevoir ce que j'appellerais le "sujet profond" de mon livre. C'est, ce sera sans doute *la rivalité du monde réel et de la représentation que nous nous en faisons.* La mainière dont le monde des apparences s'impose à nous et dont nous tentons d'imposer au monde extérieur notre interprétation particulière, fait le drame de notre vie. (p. 255)

As it is the drama behind the lives of the characters it is also par excellence Edouard's personal struggle which lies at the very heart of his own contradictory nature. On the one hand he claims to wait for reality to dictate to him, on the other hand he cannot accept the reality of what happens. The very struggle which Edouard professes to depict in the novel is taking place between the irreconcilable exigencies of his own nature.

No matter where we start out from we are continuously brought back to the novel's fundamental theme: the problem of reality. The problem of reality consists of the realist's effort to grasp it, the artist's effort to portray it, the hypocrite's effort to mask it, the counterfeiter's effort to dissimulate it, the mystic's effort to ignore it, the neurotic's effort to escape it, and the idealist's effort to sublimate it.

As we have seen in story and plot the way man perceives reality depends upon what he is; what man does with the reality he sees depends basically on his own system of values — the values he attributes to material things, to ideas, to a person, and the values he attributes to art. In turn what man is and his system of values depend on the reality around him, his environment and the forces that shape him, even when he is not aware of the nature of those forces. Man's system of values is created by what he believes he is, but, as we have seen in the themes of the plot, what he believes himself to be and what he *is* are two very different things.

When Bronja and Boris are playing together he asks her why she does not believe him. She replies that she believes him "quand c'est vrai". To which Boris objects: "Comment sais-tu quand c'est vrai" (p. 218)? How, indeed, is truth discernable in a world where reality depends on subjective values? The themes of man's attempt to see reality and the inability of some to perceive it are carried by several different component motifs.

The motif of actual physical blindness becomes an image for moral and intellectual blindness when Armand describes Rachel's diminishing vision:

> Rachel, ma soeur aînée, devient aveugle. Sa vue a beaucoup baissé ces derniers temps. Depuis deux ans elle ne peut plus lire sans lunettes. J'ai cru d'abord qu'elle n'avait qu'à changer de verres. Ça ne suffisait pas. Sur ma prière, elle a été consulter un spécialiste. Il paraît que c'est la sensibilité rétinienne qui faiblit. Tu comprends *qu'il y a là deux choses très différentes: d'une part une défectueuse accommodation du cristallin, à quoi les verres remédient.* Mais, même après qu'ils ont écarté ou rapproché l'image visuelle, celle-ci peut *impressionner insuffisamment la rétine et cette image n'être plus transmise que confusément au cerveau.* Suis-je clair? Tu ne connais presque pas Rachel; par conséquent, ne va pas croire que je cherche à t'apitoyer sur son sort. Alors, pourquoi est-ce que je te raconte tout cela?... Parce que, réfléchissant à son cas, je me suis avisé que *les idées, tout comme les images, peuvent se présenter au cerveau plus ou moins nettes.* Un esprit obtus ne reçoit que des aperceptions confuses; mais, à cause de cela même, il ne se rend pas nettement compte qu'il est obtus. Il ne commencerait à souffrir de sa bêtise que s'il *prenait conscience de cette bêtise*; et pour qu'il en prenne conscience, il faudrait qu'il devienne intelligent. Or, imagine un instant ce monstre: un imbécile assez intelligent pour comprendre nettement qu'il est bête. (pp. 357-358)[1]

This passage conveys the theme that there are two kinds of blindness — the perceptual and the conceptual. The actual percep-

---
[1] Italics are mine unless otherwise indicated.

tion of reality can be impaired in which case the individual does not see the reality around him. On the other hand the individual may actually perceive the way things are, but misinterpret them. He is then suffering from conceptual blindness. Such is Armand's plight. He claims he is the imbecile he describes. Thematically we are also reminded of the obtuseness we encountered with the old La Pérouse couple. Monsieur La Pérouse complains of his wife:

> Ses jugements sont tous faussés. Ainsi, tenez; je m'en vais vous faire comprendre: Vous savez que les images du dehors arrivent renversées dans notre cerveau, où un appareil nerveux les redresse. Eh bien, madame La Pérouse, elle, n'a pas d'appareil rectificateur. Chez elle, tout reste à l'envers. Vous jugez si c'est pénible. (p. 202)

Earlier Edouard had remarked of Madame La Pérouse: "quelle ombre monstrueuse la réalité projetait sur la paroi de cet étroit cerveau. Mais le vieux de son côté ne mésinterprétait-il pas tous les soins, toutes les attentions de la vieille, qui se croyait martyre, et dont il se faisait un bourreau" (p. 199)?

The old couple is the most obvious case of blindness, but most of the characters either cannot see reality or refuse to see it at one time or another. Blindness keeps them from seeing each other, but also from seeing themselves as they really are. Edouard carries the problem of his own reality so far that he begins to doubt his very existence:

> Il me semble parfois que je n'existe pas vraiment, mais simplement que j'imagine que je suis. Ce à quoi je parviens le plus difficilement à croire, c'est à ma propre réalité. (p. 90)

Bernard, whom Edouard calls the realist, approaches the problem of reality through the kind of reasoning typical of Cartesian philosophy:

> ...pensez-vous qu'il y ait rien, sur cette terre, qui ne puisse être mis en doute? ...C'est au point que je doute si l'on ne pourrait prendre le doute même comme point d'appui; car, enfin, lui du moins, je pense, ne nous fera jamais défaut. Je puis douter de la réalité de tout, mais pas de la réalité de mon doute. (p. 243)

Doubting all Bernard must seek his own reality within himself. Reality becomes relative to the perceiver, hence to grasp reality objectively is to accept its subjective limitations. Since there can be no absolute criteria for evaluating reality Bernard recognizes:

> ...que rien n'est bon pour tous, mais seulement par rapport à certains; que rien n'est vrai pour tous mais seulement par rapport à qui le croit tel; qu'il n'est ni méthode ni théorie qui soit applicable à chacun. (p. 245)

The absence of absolute criteria is concretely illustrated by the juxtaposition of Bernard and Boris. Both are illegitimate; both should be unhampered by seeking to conform to an hereditary prejudice; both share the same room; both have opportunities to sign their lives away in an absolute commitment. But only one does; the other refrains. Bernard fights an angel while Boris seeks desperately to see one. Yet the one who fights the angel is the realist; the one who cannot see one is the neurotic. Bernard is left to develop his own strength; Boris is treated as too weak to face reality. Madame Sophroniska says of him: "...des âmes comme celle de Boris et de Bronja ne peuvent se passer d'un aliment chimérique" (p. 262). The themes of remaining within a dream-world and its counterpart, rejection of a dream-world, are carried by two component motifs correlative by contrast:

> Boris, devant moi, rêve à voix haute. Il accepte tous les matins, de demeurer, une heure durant, dans cet état de demi-sommeil où les images qui se proposent à nous échappent au contrôle de la raison. (p. 223)

In contrast the chapter which begins with the Shakespearean quote "We are all bastards" continues:

> Bernard a fait un rêve absurde. Il ne se souvient pas de ce qu'il a rêvé. Il ne cherche pas à se souvenir de son rêve, mais à en sortir. Il rentre dans le monde réel pour sentir le corps d'Olivier peser lourdement contre lui. (p. 70)

Each boy's approach to reality is correlative by contrast. Bernard seeks to grasp its ever-changing aspect; Boris seeks to escape it into some dream-world all his own. That both Madame Sophroniska, the psychiatrist, and Edouard the eager friend, make matters worse for Boris is part of the tragic irony which pervades the whole work. Tragic irony itself is based on the unfortunate consequences which occur when reality is not perceived or misinterpreted. Tragic irony causes Azaïs to offer up a prayer of blessing for the cruel efforts of the boys' gang which he mistakes for idealistic fervor. Tragic irony causes La Pérouse to keep the gun loaded as a constant reminder that he is merely "un jouet entre les mains de Dieu". Like the Delphian oracle reality may seem unmistakable until the actual events turn its meaning upside down.

Conscious and Unconscious Blindness

There is a conscious and unconscious blindness in the face of reality. Initially unconscious blindness may progressively become awareness, whereas an initially conscious escape from reality, out of force or habit, may become unconscious. Passavant assumes a rôle in the beginning which he cannot leave even when he thinks he does.

> Il éprouva le besoin de mettre un temps et pour ainsi dire: *de quitter son rôle*, à la manière d'un acteur bien assuré de tenir son public, désireux de se prouver et de lui prouver qu'il le tient. (p. 194)

What Passavant does not realize is that while he is affecting to leave his rôle he is still playing one, especially since by these very meanderings Vincent realizes that Passavant is not to be taken seriously. As Bernard remarks: "On veut donner le change et l'on s'occupe tant de paraître, qu'on finit par ne plus savoir qui l'on est..." (p. 251).

Azaïs and his son-in-law Vedel have walled themselves off from reality of professional necessity. Of Azaïs Edouard remarks:

> A mesure qu'une âme s'enfonce dans la dévotion, elle perd le sens, le goût, le besoin, l'amour de la réalité. J'ai également observé cela chez Vedel, si peu que j'aie pu lui parler. L'éblouissement de leur foi les aveugle sur le monde qui les entoure, et sur eux-mêmes. (p. 134)

Of Vedel Armand says:

> Monsieur mon père a arrangé sa vie de telle façon qu'il n'ait plus le droit ni le moyen de ne pas l'être. [un convaincu] Oui, c'est un convaincu professionnel. Un professeur de conviction. Il inculque la foi; c'est là sa raison d'être; c'est le rôle qu'il assume et qu'il doit mener jusqu'au bout.... Il s'imagine qu'il croit, parce qu'il continue à agir comme s'il croyait. Il n'est plus libre de ne pas croire. (pp. 466-467)

As we noticed earlier the way man sees reality depends on what he is as well as his system of values. The initial choice of profession was for both Vedel and Azaïs an adoption of a system of values as well as an assumption of rôles which, once the commitment made, allowed the individual no freedom to change, unless he were willing to give up his very livelihood. The rôle then becomes instinctive as necessary a commodity for survival as food and drink. Their blindness progressively expels all problematical questions from their consciousness which would tend to place their assumed identities in doubt.

The dilemma of the old piano teacher La Pérouse is correlative by contrast and similarity. He experiences a gradual awakening, a progressive awareness of reality, which is emphasized by the linking phrase "je commence à comprendre." But in the course of the novel his growing comprehension changes into the phrase "je ne parviens pas à comprendre."

> Tenez: il y a certains actes de ma vie passée que *je commence seulement à comprendre*. Oui, *je commence seulement à comprendre* qu'ils n'ont pas du tout la signification que je croyais jadis, en les faisant.... C'est maintenant seulement que *je comprends* que toute ma vie j'ai été dupe. (p. 149)

And:

> *Je ne comprenais pas* qu'en croyant me libérer je devenais de plus en plus esclave de mon orgueil... (p. 151)

But similar to Passavant's seemingly conscious assumption of rôles and its later spurious rejection La Pérouse has left one illusion to fall into another. Edouard has come to visit him:

LUX ET VERITAS

> "—Vous avez de la fièvre? lui demandai-je.
> "Ma phrase le rappela au *sentiment de son personnage*:
> "—Monsieur de La Pérouse n'a pas de fièvre. Il n'a plus rien. Depuis mercredi soir, monsieur de La Pérouse a cessé de vivre.
> "J'hésitais si le mieux n'était pas d'entrer dans son jeu:
> "—N'est-ce pas précisément mercredi que le petit Boris est venu vous voir?
> "Il tourna la tête vers moi; un sourire comme l'ombre de celui d'autrefois, au nom de Boris, éclaira ses traits, et *consentant enfin à quitter son rôle*:
> "—Mon ami, je puis bien vous le dire à vous: ce mercredi, c'était le dernier jour qui me restait. (p. 309)

His earlier assurance is weakening. After having seen Boris he thinks God has answered his prayer:

> ...j'ai cru qu'il m'approuvait. Oui, j'ai cru cela. *Je n'ai pas compris tout de suite* qu'il se moquait de moi, comme toujours. (p. 310)

Describing his failure to actually commit suicide he exclaims: "Que s'est-il passé? *Je ne parviens pas à comprendre*" (p. 311). Gradually he explains it by his cowardice, his fear of noise, his lack of freedom. Abdication of free will becomes the only possible explanation acceptable to his distorted view of reality:

> *J'ai compris* que ce que nous appelons notre volonté, ce sont les fils qui font marcher la marionnette, et que Dieu tire. (p. 312)

He lives with this fruitless conviction until a strange noise in the wall, rationally inexplicable, causes him to exclaim to Edouard:

> Vous pourrez peut-être me dire ce que c'est... Moi, *je ne parviens pas à comprendre*. (p. 448)

In his neurotic desire to explain everything he cannot accept the mysterious. Shortly thereafter his uncertainty is climaxed by the frightening reality of Boris's death, also rationally inexplicable. The noise in the wall has disappeared. La Pérouse reflects:

> Mais je pense qu'il y a des choses que, pendant la vie, *nous ne parvenons pas à entendre*, des harmonies... parce

que ce bruit les couvre. Oui, je pense que ce n'est qu'après la mort que *nous pourrons entendre vraiment*. (p. 493)

The verb "entendre" can be used synonymously with "comprendre." The linking phrase, therefore, calls our attention to the real meaning of La Pérouse's statement. Noise is a simile for life; death will bring silence. Noise covers the harmonies he yearns for; life remains the eternal struggle with conflicting realities. We shall return to the important motifs of noise and dissonance in another context. For the moment we must analyze the implications of this linking phrase for the comprehension of La Pérouse's predicament. A reality acceptable to La Pérouse's consciousness must be harmonious, cleansed of dissonance, a reality he could *understand*. Therefore, his growing awareness of reality consists of his gradual recognition that reality is incomprehensible. He cannot, however, accept this as part of life and projects all explanations of reality into the realm of eschatology. His hovering between consciousness and unconsciousness, between recogniton of suffering and evil and indifferent though not blissful ignorance, is illustrated by his ambiguous state when he suffers from apparent insomnia. Sleep becomes a linking image for unawareness. La Pérouse explains:

> Quand il m'arrive de m'endormir, je ne perds pas le sentiment de mon sommeil. Ce n'est pas vraiment dormir, n'est-ce pas? Celui qui dort vraiment ne sent pas qu'il dort; simplement à son reveil, il s'aperçoit qu'il a dormi. (p. 447)

He is afraid of his growing awareness. His death-wish is motivated by his desire for complete peace, while his inability to kill himself stems from his fear that death could mean total awareness:

> Oui! mais la mort, je l'espère comme un sommeil; et une détonation, cela n'endort pas: cela réveille.... Oui, c'est certainement cela dont j'avais peur, au lieu de m'endormir, de me réveiller brusquement. (p. 312)

Within the theme of blindness and awareness we have seen that Bronja and Boris are deliberately kept in a dream-world, and we have observed several cases of blindness of which Edouard's and La Pérouse's are accompanied by the additional folly of vascillating between explanations of reality and the rejection of their explanations. Passavant, Azaïs, and Vedel progressively lose sight of reality to such an extent that they are oblivious to the fact that they are playing rôles.

There is also a conscious rejection of reality. Reality is perceived, but purposely rejected, because of the consequences accepted reality would entail. Pauline, to Edouard's surprise, is more aware of what is going on in her household than anyone realizes. Actually confronting her children and husband with what she knows, would, in her estimation, cause them to dissimulate all the more. Her resignation includes being resigned to knowing and not letting on that she does:

> J'ai restreint mon bonheur; d'année en année j'ai dû en rabattre; une à une, j'ai raccourci mes espérances. J'ai cédé; j'ai toléré; *j'ai feint de ne pas comprendre, de ne pas voir...* (p. 399)

By a different method, taught by life's experiences, she has arrived at Bernard's conclusion on the impossibility of knowing in the absolute:

> Dans la vie, rien ne se résout; tout continue. On demeure dans l'incertitude; et on restera jusqu'à la fin sans savoir à quoi s'en tenir; *en attendant la vie continue, continue, tout comme si de rien n'était....* (p. 400)

This passage reminds us by the affinity of the theme it conveys of Bernard's theory that doubt itself is the only thing that can be considered real. Bernard, however, of his own admission is a novice who knows nothing about life when he discusses these ideas with Laura. Life will teach him to confront a reality quite different from his expectations. What he has formulated in theory he finds hard to accept in practice after his night with Sarah:

> Il s'efforce de ne point penser, gêné de devoir incorporer cette nuit sans précédent, aux précédents de son histoire. Non; c'est un appendice, une annexe, qui ne peut trouver place, dans le corps du livre — livre où *le récit de sa vie, comme si de rien n'était va continuer, n'est-ce pas va reprendre?* (p. 383)

Nevertheless Bernard will have to incorporate this experience into the reality of his life, even though life continues "comme si de rien n'était." This fact makes the assumption of an attitude in the face of life a necessary expedience. Pauline prefers peace in her household to the revelation of disturbing realities. She sacrifices her happiness and personal recognition for the welfare of her family. Refusal to exploit reality, conscious blindness, can therefore be an act of charity, purely altruistic in intent. In this case conscious blindness has a constructive purpose. By contrast Armand's consciousness of his own plight and his refusal to do anything about it lacks any constructive purpose whatsoever. Paralyzed by the constant observation of the dichotomy between profession and actual expression in the lives of those he sees around him his deliberate blindness becomes a destructive force.

Man begins to suffer from the discrepancy between reality and his illusions only when he becomes aware that they are at odds with each other. Rejection of reality in many cases does not come from a deliberate desire to be false, but arises out of the psychological necessity to avoid pain. Escapism, mysticism, neurosis... are defense mechanisms employed to protect us from a painful reality. We have seen neurotic escapism in Boris. But escapism is indulged in by nearly every one at one time or another. It is a matter of preferring ignorance to a knowledge which would entail consequences which we do not feel capable of facing. This is the reason behind Judge Profitendieu's cautious procedures in the case of the young criminals. He does not want to arrest the culprits prematurely, because "une instruction ne peut pas revenir en arrière et que nous nous trouvons *forcés de savoir ce que nous préférerions parfois ignorer*" (p. 425). Similarly after Boris's death Ghéridanisol who had planned the disaster with malice of forethought is seized by convulsions which Rachel interprets as proof of his innocence. "*On préfère tout supposer, plutôt que l'inhumanité d'un être si jeune*; et lorsque Ghéridanisol protesta de son innocence on le crut" (p. 490).

Life is full of moments when to escape reality becomes an expedient necessity for life to go on. To dwell on man's inhumanity to man, to live in a morbid preoccupation with death, suffering, and sin is as much a distortion of reality as to ignore their existence altogether. A view of reality includes the view of a higher reality; it includes the dreams and visions which have sustained mankind in its most noble endeavors. Idealism and mysticism have their place in a realistic view of life, but only if they are counterbalanced by their complements in facts.

Apollo and Daphne

Gide uses the term "mystique" and "mysticisme" in several different contexts and calls such diverse personalities as Madame Sophroniska and Strouvilhou mystics. A mystic is one who believes in the virtue of ideas and their propelling force. Madame Sophroniska says in an "élan de mysticisme": "Je crois de toute mon âme que, sans mysticisme il ne se fait ici-bas rien de grand, rien de beau" (241). Edouard has just affirmed: "Je ne suis pas mystique." Promptly thereafter Edouard makes a complete about-face:

> Comment ai-je pu acquiescer lorque Sophroniska m'a dit que je n'avais rien d'un mystique? Je suis tout prêt à reconnaître avec elle que, sans mysticisme, l'homme ne peut réussir rien de grand. (p. 256)

Six pages later Edouard brings up the subject again in relation to Boris's pursuit of imaginary possessions and Madame Sophroniska's approval of it. Again Edouard changes his mind which is extremely comical in the context within which it appears:

> Elle [Sophroniska] parle avec émotion de la piété de ces deux enfants, qui lisent ensemble l'Apocalypse, et s'exaltent, et conversent avec les anges et revêtent leur âme de suaires blancs. Comme toutes les femmes, elle est pleine de contradictions. Mais elle avait raison: je ne suis décidément pas un mystique.... (p. 262)

Mysticism means an overemphasis on the things which are not perceptible to the senses, but which are known through intuition and spiritual insight. It dwells on the incomprehensible; it formulates theories and ideologies which are often without foundation in concrete fact. When Edouard first claims he is not a mystic, denies it, and then denies his denial he is being consistent with his inconsistent view of reality. He is experiencing to the very depths of his being the dichotomy which he constantly feels and exaggerates between concrete reality and abstract reality, between fact and idea. When his vacillations lead him to stress the ideas he wishes to convey rather than the reality behind those ideas he is being a mystic and he quickly senses the exaggeration and swerves back to the opposite extreme, which results in the slavish realism he imposes upon himself precisely because it bothers him. When he describes Georges stealing the book at the shop in such minute detail he comments: "Je note tout cela par discipline et précisément parce que cela m'ennuie de le noter" (p. 108).

The entire question of the supremacy of ideas over facts or of facts over ideas becomes not only a question of art and artistic creation but a question of existential point of view. The mystic is inclined to view facts from the perspective of his preconceived ideology. He is basically an essentialist. The realist is inclined to view ideas from the perspective of the changing world of factual phenomena. He is basically an existentialist. Edouard can never quite free himself from his preconceived ideas about art and man, and his failure in both realms is the result. He is, in fact, an incurable mystic.

The mysterious Monsieur X who talks to Edouard about his novel (similar to Roger Martin du Gard with Gide), seems to recognize Edouard's difficulty:

> Beaucoup réfléchi à ce que m'a dit X. Il ne connaît rien de ma vie, mais je lui ai exposé longuement mon plan des *Faux-Monnayeurs*. Son conseil m'est toujours salutaire; car il se place à un point de vue différent du mien. *Il craint que je ne verse dans le factice et que je ne lâche le vrai sujet pour l'ombre de ce sujet dans mon cerveau.* Ce qui m'inquiète, c'est de sentir la vie (ma vie) se séparer ici de mon oeuvre, mon oeuvre s'écarter de ma vie. Mais, ceci, je n'ai pas pu le lui dire. Jusqu'à présent, comme il sied, mes goûts, mes sentiments, mes expériences personnelles alimentaient tous mes écrits; dans mes phrases les mieux construites, encore sentais-je battre mon coeur. *Désormais, entre ce que je pense et ce que je sens, le lien est rompu.* Et je doute si précisément ce n'est pas l'empêchement que j'éprouve à laisser parler aujourd'hui mon coeur qui précipite mon oeuvre dans l'abstrait et l'artificiel. En réfléchissant à ceci, la signification de la fable d'Apollon et de Daphne m'est brusquement apparue: *heureux, ai-je pensé, qui peut saisir dans une seule étreinte le laurier et l'objet même de son amour.* (pp. 114-115)

In other words the person who is at one in heart and mind is blessed with a singleness of purpose because he can embrace the abstract and concrete, idea and fact in one kiss. The fable of Apollo and Daphne becomes a linking image whose theme is the unity of the factual and ideological, of the natural and of the supernatural worlds. Such unity is a prerequisite for productivity.

When Edouard speaks of his future novel in theory the contradictions of his method are blatant. After explaining his ideas and theories Sophroniska asks:

> Ne craignez-vous pas, en quittant la réalité, de vous égarer dans des régions mortellement abstraites, et de faire un roman, non d'êtres vivants, mais d'idées? (p. 235)

Edouard's reply is typical:

> Et quand cela serait!... Les idées..., les idées, je vous l'avoue, m'intéressent plus que les hommes.... Naturellement on peut dire que nous ne les connaissons que par les hommes, de même que nous n'avons connaissance du vent que par les roseaux qu'il incline; mais tout de même le vent importe plus que les roseaux.
> —Le vent existe indépendamment des roseaux, hasarda Bernard.
> Son intervention fit rebondir Edouard, qui l'attendait déjà depuis longtemps.
> —Oui, je sais: les idées n'existent que par les hommes; mais c'est bien là le pathétique: elles vivent aux dépens d'eux. (p. 236)

Later on Edouard and Bernard take up the same theme of the realm of ideas and facts, this time in the context of Douvier's lack of lyrical inspiration or imagination. Edouard explains Douvier's inadequacy as the inadequacy which is the result of a purely factual approach to reality:

> Paul-Ambroise [Valéry] a coutume de dire qu'il ne consent à tenir compte de rien qui ne se puisse chiffrer; ce en quoi j'estime qu'il joue sur le mot "tenir compte;" car "à ce compte-là" comme on dit, on est forcé d'omettre Dieu. C'est bien là où il tend et ce qu'il désire.... Tenez: je crois que j'appelle lyrisme l'état de l'homme qui consent à se laisser vaincre par Dieu. (p. 394)

Seeing only that which can be factually accounted for is a one-sided approach to life. Ideally facts and ideas are interrelated and interdependent, and both make up reality. Human productivity and creativity depend on their reciprocal alliance. Earlier Edouard had not recognized the necessary factual basis of ideas and Bernard had. With a new conviction and authority, which Bernard correctly attributes to Olivier's presence, Edouard affirms:

> Il n'est certes pas un mouvement mystique qui n'ait son répondant matériel. Et après? L'esprit pour témoigner, ne peut point se passer de la matière. De là le mystère de l'incarnation. (p. 394)

Edouard accepts at least in theory that ideas must be clothed in reality; they must correspond to a concrete situation; they must have their basis in fact. If they do not they become extremely dangerous. The danger for the work of art is recognized by Madame Sophroniska:

> Mais vous savez dans les romans, c'est toujours dangereux de présenter des intellectuels. Ils assomment le public; on ne parvient à leur faire dire que des âneries, et, à tout ce qui les touche, ils communiquent un air abstrait. (p. 233)

Though the danger of artistic absurdities may not be ominous, the propagation of ideologies based on doctrines divorced from facts or on distorted facts has always been a threat to human society. In this context we must mention the thematically correlative episode of Strouvilhou's explanation of his despicable ideas on man. There is much validity in the reasons for his contempt for the human race and for his deploring the absence of eugenics for man as practiced for breeds of horses and rabbits. Theoretically his ideals for the betterment of humanity may even seem laudable. But there is a major obstacle: Who is to decide in practice who must survive and who must perish and by what criteria? Here is where Strouvilhou's flagitious philosophy ties in with Edouard's less offensive mysticism, and where both flounder in their moral and ethical perception of reality. Strouvilhou explains to Passavant:

> Je crains que vous ne vous soyez mépris sur moi jusqu'à présent, Monsieur le comte. Vous m'avez pris pour un

sceptique et je suis un idéaliste, un mystique. Le scepticisme n'a jamais donné rien de bon. On sait de reste où il mène... à la tolérance! Je tiens les sceptiques pour des gens sans idéal, sans imagination; pour des sots.... (p. 414)

Strouvilhou's idealism, akin to Nietzsche's ideology, is not skepticism nor nihilism, but a confidence enhanced by modern evolutionary views that humanity is perfectible, that overman could somehow emerge from the herd. The implementation of Strouvilhou's ideology would mean the domination of one part of humanity over another, whereas the need for domination paradoxically stems from weakness. This weakness comes from the incapacity to perceive the essence of reality, for domination springs from the inability to relate to the world other than by exerting power over others as though they were objects.

The presence of both worlds: the concrete world of actuality and the abstract world of ideas are necessary for productivity, because productivity is based on the interaction of both. This recognition lies at the very heart of the artistic creation. Throughout *Les Faux-Monnayeurs* the question of artistic creativity and its relation to reality is a subject of intense discussion. Edouard recognizes the grandeur of classical art in its universality expressed by the particular. Typically he overstresses the universal at the expense of the particular granting specific existence only to psychological truth: "Il n'y a de vérité psychologique que particulière, il est vrai; mais il n'y a d'art que général" (p. 231).

Just as man's perception of reality must combine the levels of the purely factual and the purely ideological, the work of art must integrate these two elements also. Its truth must be universal, its meaning general, its interpretation catholic. Its fiction, however, must be particular, its setting specific, its characters human. The ancient Greeks and the French classicists wrote such works which Edouard admires as the most human and most perfect ever written:

> Mais précisément, cela n'est humain que profondément; cela ne se pique pas de le paraître, ou du moins de paraître réel. Cela demeure une oeuvre d'art. (p. 230)

To perceive the essence of reality man must be able to see the beauty of Daphne in the laurel tree, the supernatural in the natural, the universal truth in the particular representation of reality. He must be able to penetrate the surface to visualize the substance, permeate the skin to the very essence of things.

The Counterfeit Coin

To penetrate the surface in order to visualize the substance and to permeate the skin to the very heart of reality is to be wary of surface appearances and to probe for the naked truth. The most prominent linking image of the novel conveys this theme and is illustrated by the motif of the counterfeit coin. Bernard describes it:

> Elle n'a pas tout à fait le poids, je crois, mais elle a l'éclat et presque le son d'une vraie pièce; le revêtement est en or, de sorte qu'elle vaut pourtant un peu plus de deux sous; mais elle est en crystal. A l'usage, elle va devenir transparente. Non, ne la frottez pas; vous me l'abîmeriez. Déjà l'on voit presque au travers. (p. 239)

The deceptive outer layer wears off with time and uncovers the truth underneath. As this is applied specifically to money it also applies to people, to ideas, and to words. The counterfeit coin points to the theme of authenticity. Similar to the image of the marble-top table discussed earlier which conveys the theme of the unmasking of the real nature of the characters, the image of the counterfeit coin illustrates perceptually the correlative theme that outer appearances are false and that time reveals truth.

There are many overdressed characters in *Les Faux-Monnayeurs* who in time are exposed in their nakedness. Gide demonstrates this by his subtle references to articles of clothing in significant contexts. The most striking example is the pastor. Strouvilhou cunningly makes a great fuss about Vedel's attire in the pulpit. He claims that the sight of Vedel's street suit underneath his clerical robe "était d'un fâcheux effet sur certains fidèles" (p. 129). The following Sunday Vedel tried to preach with his arms at his sides in order not to reveal the suit, and he spoiled his rhetorical effectiveness. He tried once more without the suit and caught a cold. Like the significant image conveyed in *Le Rouge et le Noir* when Julien Sorel stands at the altar with his spurs and the outline of his honor-guard uniform clearly visible underneath his soutane, Pasteur Vedel cannot preach without, to use a biblical term, the "old man" showing underneath.

The apparel of profession cannot hide the real man underneath. This theme is again conveyed when Oscar Molinier confides in Edouard and Edouard comments:

> Jusqu'à ce jour, je n'avais vu de lui que le magistrat; l'homme enfin écartait sa toge. (p. 282)

Edouard speaks of the "vêtements d'emprunt" of the person who makes himself into something he is not. The motivation behind a borrowed identity need not be founded on the desire to be deceptive at all. As Edouard shows in relation to Laura this assumed identity may be born out of love:

> Chacune de ses admirations, je le comprends aujourd'hui, n'était pour elle qu'un lit de repos où allonger sa pensée contre la mienne; rien ne répondait en ceci à l'exigence profonde de sa nature. "Je ne m'ornais et ne me parais que pour toi," disait-elle. Précisément, j'aurais voulu que ce ne fût que pour elle et qu'elle cédât, ce faisant, à quelque intime besoin personnel. Mais de tout cela, qu'elle ajoutait à elle pour moi, rien ne restera, pas même un regret, pas même le sentiment d'un manque. Un jour vient où l'être vrai reparaît, que le temps lentement déshabille de tous ses vêtements d'emprunt; et, si c'est de ces ornements que l'autre est épris, il ne presse plus contre son coeur qu'une parure déshabitée, qu'un souvenir... que du deuil et du désespoir. (pp. 88-89)

In contrast to Edouard's constant probing for the truth Passavant adopts the philosophy which Olivier later conveys to Bernard in their argument over the meaning of La Fontaine's words: "Je vais de fleur en fleur et d'objet en objet." Olivier contends:

> ...La Fontaine avait fait le portrait de l'artiste, de celui qui consent à ne prendre du monde que l'extérieur, que la surface, que la fleur. Puis j'aurais posé en regard un portrait savant, du chercheur, de celui qui creuse, et montré enfin que, pendant que le savant fonce l'artiste trouve; que celui qui s'enfonce s'aveugle; que la vérité, c'est l'apparence; que le mystère, c'est la forme, et que ce que l'homme a de plus profond, c'est sa peau. (p. 328)

Bernard becomes indignant. He knows that Olivier is just parroting Passavant, and he cannot accept the count's superficiality nor Olivier's lack of originality. Bernard's examination paper expressed the opposite view:

> J'ai dit... que le véritable esprit de la France était un esprit d'examen, de logique, d'amour et de pénétration patiente... (p. 330)

That Bernard refers to the ideals of France astonishes Olivier, but it is not really surprising in the light of his development. Using the imagery of the coin and applying it to himself Bernard explains his ambition of becoming something more than skin-deep:

> Je voudrais, tout au long de ma vie, au moindre choc, rendre un son pur, probe, authentique. Presque tous les gens que j'ai connus sonnent faux. Valoir exactement ce qu'on paraît; ne pas chercher à paraître plus qu'on ne vaut.... (p. 251)

The problem of authenticity as we have seen in the themes of the story is closely linked with the identity of the individual. For the individual to be authentically himself his identity cannot be static; his being must evolve. No absolute values can be affixed to the personality. The value of money is also flexible determined by numerous interrelated factors of the economy. Inflation, rate of change, devaluation are all part of the economic game. In human society objective though not absolute values become a necessity for social interaction. Established norms of value in ethical, moral, legal, and economic matters become a matter of convention upon which society depends. That conventions depend upon the majority to uphold them does, of course, not mean that the majority is right. This is Strouvilhou's basic argument:

> Dans un monde où chacun triche, c'est l'homme vrai qui fait figure de charlatan. (p. 415)

and indeed, there seem to be very few in *Les Faux-Monnayeurs* who do not cheat in one way or another.

By contrast Bernard learns to respect the concept and potential of conventional values when upheld by each individual. Having observed a man trying to smuggle something by the customs officials he exclaims:

> J'ai compris brusquement l'autre jour *à cette indignation qui m'a pris en entendant le touriste* de la frontière parler du plaisir qu'il avait à frauder la douane. "Voler l'Etat c'est ne voler personne," disait-il. Par protestation, j'ai compris tout à coup ce que c'était que l'Etat. Et je me suis mis à l'aimer, simplement parce qu'on lui faisait du tort. Je n'avais jamais réfléchi à cela. "L'Etat, ce n'est qu'une convention," disait-il encore. Quelle belle chose ce serait, une convention qui reposerait sur la bonne foi de chacun... si seulement il n'y avait que des gens probes. (p. 251)

Ideally conventional values would be determined by a group of upright individuals. In the absence of Utopia the values upon which society is built are not necessarily right, but accepted as right by convention. They appear to be right as the counterfeit coin appears to be authentic until time and wear reveal its transparency. Ethical, moral, and social standards are based on the values which society agrees to attribute to them. The image of the counterfeit coin is therefore not totally derogatory. By convention and social expediency values of money, people, ideas, and words are accepted as authentic until proven otherwise. The folly of our human ways is stubbornly to hold on to values which have been established as counterfeit. The best system of values provides for its own modification and change. Within this context complete adherence to past values is just as dangerous as a complete overthrow of prevailing values. Both extremes are illustrated in the novel and are correlative by contrast.

Bernard feels the same indignation he had felt about the individual tourist not respecting the values of society that he feels about the political group which is not respecting the values of the individual. The speakers of the conservative political group he visits have announced their doctrine of adhering to the past:

> ...l'orateur cependant continuait. Quand Bernard recommença de l'écouter, il enseignait un moyen certain de ne jamais se tromper, qui était de renoncer à jamais juger par soi-même, mais bien de s'en remettre toujours aux jugements de ses supérieurs.

> —Ces supérieurs, qui sont-ils? demanda Bernard; et soudain *une grande indignation s'empara de lui.* (p. 436)

Strouvilhou is the proponent of the overthrow of all values and conventions:

> A vrai dire, mon cher comte, je dois vous avouer que, de toutes les nauséabondes émanations humaines, la littérature est une de celles qui me dégoûtent le plus. Je n'y vois que complaisances et flatteries. Et j'en viens à douter qu'elle puisse devenir autre chose, du moins tant qu'elle n'aura pas balayé le passé. Nous vivons sur des sentiments admis et que le lecteur s'imagine éprouver, parce qu'il croit tout ce qu'on imprime; l'auteur spécule là-dessus comme sur des conventions qu'il croit les bases de son art. Ces sentiments sonnent faux comme des jetons, mais ils ont cours. Et, comme l'on sait que "la mauvaise monnaie chasse la bonne," celui qui offrirait au public de vraies pièces semblerait nous payer de mots. Dans un monde ou chacun triche, c'est l'homme vrai qui fait figure de charlatan. Je vous en avertis: si je dirige une revue, ce sera pour y crever des outres, pour y démonétiser tous les beaux sentiments, et ces billets à ordre: les mots.

Words like coins have conventional values. Strouvilhou wants to demonetize their accepted meanings, throw everything out, do away with the past. The result of this philosophy as we learn from the actual make-up of the review is chaos. The entire goal of collaboration on the review, called *Le fer à repasser,* is to "discréditer" all existing values, but to discredit all the values of the past is really to give equal value to the molehill and the mountain, to literally "iron" out all distinctions between greatness and banality.

To trace the future only by the norms of the past is as impossible as to live without any reference to the past whatsoever. Man does not live in a timeless vacuum, where he can ignore his spatial and temporal dimensions, i.e. his *Dasein.* Some of the characters in the novel try to cut themselves off from the past while others try to cut themselves off from the future. None of them, however, succeeds.

Cut-off Hands

The theme of rejection of the past is carried by a linking image which is placed focally within the narrative and which affects all the component motifs which carry the same theme by its vividness. This linking image is the cutting off of hands which occurs in connection with the shipwreck of *La Bourgogne*. Lilian recounts her traumatic experience:

> ...deux marins, l'un armé d'une hache et l'autre d'un couteau de cuisine... coupaient les doigts, les poignets de quelques nageurs qui, s'aidant des cordes, s'efforçaient de monter dans notre barque. (p. 80)

Lilian applies this image to the change in her life:

> ...j'ai compris que je n'étais plus, que je ne pourrais plus jamais être la même, la sentimentale jeune fille d'auparavant; j'ai compris que j'avais laissé une partie de moi sombrer avec *la Bourgogne*, qu'à un tas de sentiments délicats, désormais, je couperais les doigts et les poignets pour les empêcher de monter et de faire sombrer mon coeur. (p. 80; Gide's italics)

Here the image is used to convey the theme of cutting off sensitivity, sentimentality, and nostalgia in order to survive. The fact that she cuts herself off from the past keeps her, so she believes, from being drowned in life. Later that same day Vincent is troubled:

> Il me semble que quelque chose veut monter dans ma barque — c'est pour que tu me comprennes que je me sers de ton image — quelque chose que je veux empêcher d'y monter.... Quelque chose que je repousse, mais dont j'entends la voix... une voix que tu n'as jamais entendue; que j'écoutais dans mon enfance... (p. 181)

Lilian rebukes him: "Tu ne sais pas couper les mains proprement" (p. 183). The theme has been expressed that it is difficult to cut oneself off from one's past. But at the feet of Lilian Vincent will learn quickly. And the image reappears in Alexandre's letter about Vincent:

> ...il se croit le diable lui-même, si j'ai bien compris ce qu'il disait. Il a dû lui arriver quelque aventure, car, en rêve ou dans l'état de demi-sommeil où il lui arrive souvent de tomber (et alors il converse avec lui-même comme si je n'étais pas là), il parle sans cesse de *mains coupées*. (p. 471)

And further down:

> Il ne parle jamais de sa vie passée, de sorte que je ne parviens pas à découvrir qui ce peut être. (p. 472)

It is significant that we know that Vincent pushed Lilian off the boat into the Cassamance. The very lesson she had learned and which she deemed essential for her survival is the reason for her death. Thus the image which portrays her concept of the necessity of cutting off from the past, at the same time shows the impossibility of doing so. Even Vincent's dreams are haunted by his past. The past took revenge on Lilian, for had she not taught him to cut himself off from the past, he would not have cut himself off from her as part of his past, as she had made him cut himself off from Laura. Thus Lilian's own past has returned in the form of her own words and has taken its revenge. The actual outcome of the incidents confirms the theme that man cannot escape his past.

This very theme is announced in similar terms using the same imagery at the very beginning of the book. We are in Monsieur Profitendieu's living room. Bernard has left the letter of his departure behind, and Profitendieu is left with the task of breaking the news to his family which he finds extremely difficult:

> Il ne pouvait portant pas raconter la vérité, livrer aux enfants le secret de l'égarement passager de leur mère. Oh! Tout était si bien pardonné, oublié, réparé. La naissance d'un dernier fils avait scellé leur réconciliation. Et soudain ce spectre vengeur qui resort du passé, ce cadavre que le flot ramène... (p. 26)

Even when the past is buried, drowned along with some shipwreck, forgotten — its corpse returns washed up on the sands of our consciousness to haunt us. This is a theme of *l'Immoraliste*, this is the fallacy behind Lafcadio's *acte gratuit*, and this is why

Lilian's brave theory will not prove true. This theme is shown over and over again in the novel. Bernard cuts himself off from his past, his former life, does it consciously, but even his audacious step of leaving his family is taken with mixed emotions: ..."il était ému comme s'il prenait congé du même coup de son passé; il répéta bien vite adieu, puis partit, avant de laisser éclater le gros sanglot qui montait à sa gorge" (p. 20). Olivier, encouraged by Bernard's example, also takes off, but the ties of the past bring both of them back to the fold.

In contrast to the theme of cutting off from the past there are those in the novel who cut themselves off from the future. La Pérouse consciously ceases to live even though he cannot quite bring it over himself to discharge the pistol. Laura explains to Bernard that her failure in life stems from the moment in Pau when she cut herself off from the possibility of a future:

> Vous savez quelle a été ma faute? De ne plus en [de la vie] attendre rien. C'est quand j'ai cru, hélas! que je n'avais plus rien à attendre, que je me suis abandonnée. J'ai vécu ce printemps à Pau, comme si plus rien n'importait. Bernard, je puis vous dire, à présent que j'en suis punie: ne désespérez jamais de la vie. (p. 253)

The individual cannot ignore the temporal realities of his existence by cutting himself off from the past or from the future. Here again we arrive at the thematic conclusion of the story. A balance between absolutes becomes the only acceptable answer to the dilemma of the individual who wants to pursue his authentic identity but who at the same time must realize that he does not live in a vacuum, but in the present affected by both past and future and in a society based on norms and conventions.

The Automaton

The novel illustrates by numerous examples that artificial constraints which make man into something he is not eventually lead to catastrophe. La Pérouse vainly forces himself to become better than he is. By contrast Vincent tries to suppress his better nature. La Pérouse explains:

> Quand j'étais jeune, je menais une vie très austère; je me félicitais de ma force de caractère chaque fois que je repoussais une sollicitation. Je ne comprenais pas qu'en croyant me libérer je devenais de plus en plus esclave de mon orgueil. Chacun de ces triomphes sur moi-même, c'était un tour de clef que je donnais à la porte de mon cachot. (pp. 150-51)

Vincent also invents new ethics which are the opposite of La Pérouse's, but which lead to the same disastrous results:

> Et ce qui disposait Vincent à considérer sa façon d'agir avec Laura comme une victoire de sa volonté sur ses instincts affectifs, c'est que, naturellement bon, il avait dû se forcer, se raidir, pour se montrer dur envers elle. (p. 177)

And later:

> Renoncement au bon motif, considéré comme une duperie, à la lueur de la nouvelle éthique que Vincent se trouve devoir inventer....
> A partir de quoi, l'être qui se croit le plus libre, n'est plus qu'un instrument à son service. (p. 179)

In relation to La Pérouse the motifs of the automaton, the puppet, the wheels of a mechanism are used to illustrate that he is no longer a free individual but a machine which is set in motion by external forces over which he has no control. Similarly with Vincent the motifs of half-sleep and somnambulism are used which are repeated in connection with Boris where the analogy is carried so far that he actually kills himself by the clock.

When La Pérouse claims he is already dead Edouard describes him thus:

> Je me suis assis à côté de lui, de sorte que je ne le voyais que du profil. Ses traits restaient *durs* et *figés*. Par instants, ses lèvres s'agitaient, mais il ne disait rien. J'en venais à douter s'il me reconnaissait. La pendule a sonné quatre heures; alors, *comme mû par un rouage d'horlogerie, il a tourné la tête lentement* et d'une voix solennelle, forte mais atone et comme d'outre-tombe: "Pourquoi vous a-t-on fait entrer?... (p. 307)

Later La Pérouse describes himself as a puppet:

> Imaginez une marionnette qui voudrait quitter la scène avant la fin de la pièce ...Halte-là! On a encore besoin de vous pour la finale. Ah! vous croyiez que vous pouviez partir quand vous vouliez! ...J'ai compris que ce que nous appelons notre volonté, ce sont les fils qui font marcher la marionnette et que Dieu tire. (p. 312)

The frequent use of the verb "se figer" emphasizes immobility, the absence of life. The following passage from Edouard's first visit to La Pérouse is significant:

> Malgré le bruit voisin de la rue, le calme de cette petite pièce me paraissait extraordinaire, et malgré la lueur du réverbère qui nous éclairait fantastiquement de bas en haut à la manière d'une rampe de théâtre, les pans d'ombre, aux côtés de la fenêtre, semblaient gagner et les ténèbres, autour de nous, *se figer, comme par un grand froid, se fige une eau tranquille; se figer jusque dans mon coeur.* (p. 151)

The growing shadows engulf both of them and become tangible and concrete, something that hardens like the heart at death.

The same paralysis which kept him from killing himself prevents him from stopping Boris's suicide:

> ...soudain il reconnut le pistolet; Boris venait de le porter à sa tempe. La Pérouse comprit et *sentit aussitôt un grand froid, comme si le sang figeait dans ses veines.* Il voulut se lever, courir à Boris, le retenir, crier... Une sorte de râle rauque sortit de ses lèvres; *il resta figé, paralytique,* secoué d'un grand tremblement. (p. 489)

When man is reduced to a robot-like mechanism his actions are merely the result of an accumulated momentum. The spring is wound up ready to uncoil toward its inevitable destination. Unwittingly Madame Sophroniska reduces Boris to such an automaton. The very method of psychological penetration she employs lays bare the mechanism of his tormented soul. Edouard describes her method:

> Le pauvre enfant n'a plus en lui le moindre taillis, la moindre touffe où s'abriter des regards de la doctoresse.

> Il est tout débusqué. Sophroniska étale au grand jour, démontés, *les rouages les plus intimes de son organisme mental, comme un horloger les pièces de la pendule qu'il nettoie*. Si, après cela, le petit *ne sonne pas à l'heure*, c'est à y perdre son latin. (p. 256)

In the perspective of the lugubrious count-down toward the moment of death which Boris passively submits to these words take on all the forcefulness of tragic irony. He will indeed function as the clock the psychiatrist has made him become.

> Boris s'avança donc jusqu'à la place marquée. Il marchait à pas lents, *comme un automate, le regard fixe; comme un somnambule plutôt*. (p. 488)

The inevitability of the tragedy lies not only in the temporal but also in the spatial restriction:

> La place fatale était, je l'ai dit, contre la porte condamnée qui formait, à droite de la chaire, un retrait... (p. 488)

Significantly a door was there suggesting that there might have been an alternative for Boris, yet ironically that door had been condemned. It was, of course, not Boris's fault that this door had been condemned, that Madame Sophroniska had helped him become a human machine, that Edouard had placed him in the stifling environment of the Vedel-Azaïs pension. Boris is a toy of fate, and his tragic end is in great part due to the forces of a hostile environment over which he has no control.

The Wilting Flower

The theme of the influence of environment is a dominant theme of the book. We remember Edouard's remark against families and their "régime cellulaire". It is not happenstance that Gide makes his hero Bernard a bastard and juxtaposes him to the other bastard Boris. The forces that shape the individual are far more complex than the familiar disputes over heredity and environment. Oscar Molinier's complacent view of the determining power of heredity arises out of his ignorance as to the true nature of his own sons. Gide obviously rejected such determinism because it would rule out the possibility of the individual development of identity. For each individual there is a path on the ocean of life, but man is not alone on that ocean and is daily subjected to the waves of others and the winds of change. Sometimes it does not take much to lead an individual off course, in fact, in a significant episode of the novel a mere penetrating look makes young Georges Molinier do the opposite of what he had intended.

We are constantly acting and reacting in relation to our environment. The stifling spatial restriction which Boris experiences is part of the theme of environment announced earlier in Edouard's Journal:

> Les romanciers nous abusent losqu'ils développent l'individu sans tenir compte des compressions d'alentour. *La forêt façonne l'arbre.* A chacun si peu de place est laissée! Que de bourgeons atrophiés! Chacun lance où il peut sa ramure. La branche mystique, le plus souvent, c'est à de l'étouffement qu'on la doit. On ne peut échapper qu'en hauteur. (p. 345)

Although these words refer to Pauline's resignation and remind us of a corresponding passage concerning Madame Vedel of whom he says: "elle prend élan sur le retrécissement de son sol" (p. 297), it is most strikingly correlative with the effects of the environment on Boris. Surrounded by the "atmosphère austère" of the pension on one side and by the wickedness of his schoolmates on the other the actual spatial dimension of his "breathing room" diminishes progressively until it finally dwindles to a mere patch on the floor marked off by chalk.

The basic characteristic of the environment of the pension is its stifling, asphixiating quality. Olivier is surprised that Edouard had once been a *pensionnaire* and asks: "Et vous n'étouffiez pas dans l'atmosphère de cette boîte" (p. 125)? Edouard describes it:

> Odeur puritaine très spéciale. L'exhalaison est aussi forte, et peut-être plus asphixiante encore, dans les meetings catholiques ou juifs.... (p. 127)

He makes the following description of Azaïs' room:

> L'atmosphère de la pièce était si austère qu'il semblait que des fleurs dussent y faner aussitôt. (p. 132)

Just as the flower fades and dies in such an atmosphere Boris seems to wilt away. The reference to the wilting flower reminds us of the biological imagery used by Edouard in his description of environment. The relevance of drawing parallels between the world of nature and the world of man had been pointed to earlier by Vincent:

> Il n'est pas de grande découverte en zootechnie qui n'ait eu son retentissement dans la connaissance de l'homme. Tout cela se touche et se tient; et je crois que ce n'est jamais impunément qu'un romancier, qui se pique d'être psychologue, détourne les yeux du spectacle de la nature et reste ignorant de ses lois. (p. 187)

Carrying the analogy to its conclusion we are brought back to the theme of the development of the individual identity. Vincent comments that in nature even the weak and recalcitrant plants can be made to bear fruit by pruning and that an audacious horticulturist had once deliberately selected the weakest plants to breed hybrids with the result that they carried the most beautiful blossoms:

> Puis Vincent parla de la sélection. Il exposa la méthode ordinaire des obtenteurs pour avoir les plus beaux semis, leur choix des spécimens les plus robustes, et cette fantaisie expérimentale d'un horticulteur audacieux qui, par horreur de la routine, l'on dirait presque par défi, s'avisa d'élire au contraire les individus les plus débiles, —et les floraisons incomparables qu'il obtint. (pp. 188-189)

Had Boris's "mystic" branches been pruned or the trees around him thinned out to give him more room nature of herself might have brought Boris to fruition.

Salt and Light

That which deprives man of his natural tendencies, which keeps him from his potential as an individual, are those forces which would reduce him to the subhuman or raise him to the superhuman. Both mean a loss of a human dimension which results in tragedy. This theme is announced at the beginning of Edouard's

Journal after his first visit to La Pérouse. Here he expounds his concept of the real nature of the tragic:

> Une sorte de tragique a jusqu'à présent, me semble-t-il, échappé presque à la littérature. Le roman s'est occupé des traverses du sort, de la fortune bonne ou mauvaise, des rapports sociaux, du conflit des passions, des caractères, mais point de *l'essence même de l'être*.
> Transporter le drame sur le plan moral, c'était pourtant l'effort du christianisme. Mais il n'y a pas, à proprement parler, de romans chrétiens. Il y a ceux qui se proposent des fins d'édification; mais cela n'a rien à voir avec ce que je veux dire. Le tragique moral — qui, par exemple, fait si formidable la parole évangélique: "Si le sel perd sa saveur, avec quoi la lui rendra-t-on?" C'est ce tragique-là qui m'importe. (p. 156)

The real tragic for man lies in the loss of his very essence, of his humanity, of that which distinguishes him from the animal-like creature Vincent has become and from the vegetable-like creature La Pérouse has become, and of that which distinguishes man from overman. We have seen the tragic result of the automaton-man. Gide hints at the tragic of an overman in the very diabolical nature of Strouvilhou's presence. The supercession of the human species would really mean that man as man will have lost his significance, and will have become a mere by-passed link in the course of evolutionary change. Man's potential lies rather in a comprehension of a new humanism, in the very essence of what makes him human.

The theme of man's essence in relation to his environment is carried by the motifs of salt and light. In the Scripture passage Edouard refers to, Christ's pronouncement "Ye are the salt of the earth, and if the salt lose its savor wherewith shall it be salted", is directly followed by "Ye are the light of the world". In the biblical context salt and light are used as images to portray the nature and attributes of the one who becomes part of God's kingdom.

Within the context of perceiving truths for humanity in the infinite variety of nature Vincent tells his "fish stories". He speaks of the fish who weaken in a certain environment and who are then devoured by those who have the capacity to adapt themselves to varied environments:

> A part certaines régions, reprit Vincent, ce degré de salaison est à peu près constant; et la faune marine ne supporte d'ordinaire que des variations de densité très faibles. Mais les régions dont je parlais ne sont pourtant pas inhabitées; ce sont celles sujettes à d'importantes évaporations, qui réduisent la quantité de l'eau par rapport à la proportion de sel, ou celles au contraire où un apport constant d'eau douce dilue le sel et, pour ainsi dire, dessale la mer — celles voisines des embouchures des grands fleuves, ou de tels énormes courants comme celui que l'on appelle le Gulf Stream. Dans ces régions, les animaux dits *sténohalins* languissent et en viennent à périr; et, comme ils sont alors incapables de se défendre contre les animaux dits *euryhalins*, dont ils deviennent inévitablement la proie, les *euryhalins* vivent de préférence sur les confins des grands courants, où la densité des eaux change, là où viennent agoniser les *sténohalins*. (pp. 189-190; italics Gide's)

In the laws of natural selection the strong devour the weak just as the members of the "confrérie des hommes forts" set about destroying the weaker Boris who had lost his capacity to adapt to an environment which had deprived him of his essence.

The most impressive linking image of the entire novel is to be found in Vincent's second fish story which describes the fish who project their own light:

> La lumière du jour, vous le savez sans doute, ne pénètre pas très avant dans la mer. Ses profondeurs sont ténébreuses... abîmes immenses, que longtemps on a pu croire inhabités; puis les dragages qu'on a tentés ont ramené de ces enfers quantité d'animaux étranges. Ces animaux étaient aveugles, pensait-on. Qu'est-il besoin du sens de la vue, dans le noir? Evidemment, ils n'avaient point d'yeux; ils ne pouvaient pas, ils ne devaient pas en avoir. Pourtant on les examine, et l'on constate, avec stupeur, que certains ont des yeux; qu'ils en ont presque tous, sans compter, parfois même en sus, des antennes d'une sensibilité prodigieuse. On veut douter encore; on s'émerveille: pourquoi des yeux, pour ne rien voir? des yeux sensibles, mais sensibles à quoi?... Et voici qu'on découvre enfin que chacun de ces animaux, que d'abord on voulait

obscurs, émet et projette devant soi, à l'entour de soi, *sa lumière. Chacun d'eux éclaire, illumine, irradie.* Quand la nuit, ramenés du fond de l'abîme, on les versait sur le pont du navire, la nuit était éblouie. Feux mouvants, vibrants, versicolores, phares tournants, scintillement d'astres, de pierreries, dont rien, nous disent ceux qui les ont vus, ne saurait égaler la splendeur. (pp. 190-191; italics Gide's)

Man lives in a world of darkness, of gathering shadows. He stumbles up against the inevitable limitations of his being — his inability to see truth and reality in the absolute. Yet why does he have eyes to see if he is constantly brought up against a wall of darkness? If man is to be so limited in his ultimate capacity for perceiving the truth, why did the Creator endow him with the consciousness of the existence of an absolute which would forever escape his grasp?

Thematically the problem has been stated in all the passages I quoted in relation to blindness and unawareness and man's struggle to grasp reality. When we go back over these passages in the light of this linking image we discern that they all carried the theme of the problem of our human condition. The solution which Gide offers and which in turn is confirmed by an intricate correlation of themes is that man must project his own light. Within the limitations of his being, the darkness of his surroundings, the changeability of his identity, and the uncertainty of his destiny man must live according to the resources he finds within himself. These resources, this light, constitute the essence of man, his very humanity. Bernard is the one who finds this truth. He discovers the truth that the path of his life must be determined by the ever-changing necessity of his being — "de trouver cette règle en soi-même; d'avoir comme but le développement de soi" (p. 442). His own self-realization becomes a self-transcendence, that is, he must indeed follow his inclinations provided they lead upward. Progress is not denied the human race. The image of the fish projecting their own light conveys the theme that man may evolve from the depths of darkness by following his own light "pourvu que cela soit en montant".

In this context Bernard's rejection of exterior guidelines for a goal in his life takes on added significance. The orator of the political conservative party used identical imagery to convey the opposite theme — rejection of all individuality:

> ...Un autre orateur ...s'éleva contre le présomptueux qui prétend vivre sans doctrine, ou se guider lui-même et d'après *ses propres clartés*. (p. 434)

Presumptuous though it may be, to live according to one's own "clartés" becomes the only answer acceptable to the individual who has become aware that no ready-made formulas can be imposed on his life.

Life is an eternal struggle between man's awareness of his limitations and his efforts to overcome them. This tension in our human condition is reality itself, and all efforts to resolve that tension turn out to be fraudulent attempts to deprive man of the very essence of his humanity. We are brought back to the motifs of noise and disharmony which carry the theme of the reality of life and their opposites, silence and harmony, which convey lifelessness and death.

The tensions, polarities of life are too disturbing for La Pérouse to accept. He cannot admire that which troubles him. That is why he cannot appreciate *Hernani* or modern music. Edouard points out the logical result of his objection to disharmony:

> Vous ne prétendez pourtant pas restreindre la musique à la seule expression de la sérénité? Dans ce cas, un seul accord suffirait: un accord parfait continu. (p. 208)

This idea transfigures the old man's face with a glow of ecstasy. Perfect harmony, serenity, a perfect continuous chord, are the very assurances he longs for. He does not realize until later that such harmony means death:

> ...je pense qu'il y a des choses que, pendant la vie, nous ne parvenons pas à entendre, des harmonies ...parce que ce bruit les couvre. Oui, je pense que ce n'est qu'après la mort que nous pourrons entendre vraiment. (p. 493)

The reason for our incapacity to hear harmony, he asserts, lies in the fact that the noise of the devil drowns out the word of God. Finally, within the logic of his argument he must reject the dichotomy between good and evil and reduce God to the level of the devil:

> Non! Non! s'écria-t-il confusément; le diable et le bon Dieu ne font qu'un; ils s'entendent. (p. 494)

The final reduction of the polarities of existence to absolute harmony results in the identification of good with evil and the negation of life itself.

Such harmony in the end is sham and mockery. Man's attempt to do away with the very dissonnance of existence deprives him of his authenticity and makes him counterfeit. The desire for absolute harmony leads merely to a deafness which covers up evil, and to a blindness which shuts its eyes to reality. It is the recognition of the existence of evil, however, which uncovers the sham and lays bare the naked truth of our human condition. There is no Rousseauist peace in nature. Strouvilhou has no illusions:

> La grande paix que les philanthropes eux-mêmes prétendent puiser dans la contemplation de la nature, faune et flore, vient de ce qu'à l'état sauvage, seuls les êtres robustes prospèrent; tout le reste, déchet, sert d'engrais. *Mais on ne sait pas voir cela; on ne veut pas le reconnaître!* (p. 413)

In the darkness of man's ignorance the light of awareness emerged with the knowledge of evil. Man's condition is still limited by his ignorance, but now he knows that he does not know. He cannot return to his initial state of innocence in some symbolical Garden of Eden. He must forever strive onward and upward — guided by his own light.

CONCLUSION

It is the mystery of great art that no single approach or method can possibly exhaust its riches. Having indicated some of the major motifs and themes and their interrelationships I am aware that there are numerous themes which have been under-emphasized or omitted. As complex an interrelationship of themes as those pertaining to our human condition cannot be reduced to a few simple images or axioms.

It was my objective to demonstrate that *Les Faux-Monnayeurs* presents an intricate pattern of themes which form a coherent, harmonious whole. The complexity of the story and plot, the multiplicity of characters, and the structural problems tend to obscure the underlying unity of the novel. We have, however, by virtue of a "distanciated" perspective been able to see the linear progression of the themes of the story, the cause-effect relationships of the themes of the plot, and the generic coherence of themes based on component motifs.

In the themes of the story we discerned that the characters in *Les Faux-Monnayeurs* are faced with the problem of their attitude toward life, of their identity in relationship to others, to their destiny, and to the world, and that they all fail to find an absolute truth to live by. In the themes of the plot we discovered that man is shaped by irrational forces whose origins and effects he does not understand, but that if he is to avoid becoming a counterfeiter he must develop his own individuality provided this development is not harmful to others. Finally, in the generic coherence of themes we have seen that our limited human condition constitutes man's curse as well as his blessing; it forces man to cope with the meaning of his existence. He cannot return to a prehuman state of harmony with nature, nor can he predetermine his destiny. He has become the eternal wanderer, expelled from paradise, who is forced to go forward without the certainty of an absolute. Like Faust man is compelled to strive eternally with unceasing effort. Therein lies his strength and victory. When Sorge blinds Faust, he is still undaunted:

> Die Nacht scheint tiefer tief hereinzudringen,
> Allein im Innern leuchtet helles Licht...

On the level of themes great works resemble each other.

BIBLIOGRAPHY

Albérès, René Marill. *Histoire du roman moderne.* Paris: Albin Michel, 1962.
Aristotle. *On Poetry and Style.* Translated by G. M. A. Grube. New York: The Liberal Arts Press.
Booth, Wayne C. "Distance and Point-of-View: An Essay in Classification." *Theory of the Novel,* ed. Philip Stevick. New York: Free Press, 1967.
Brée, Germaine. *André Gide, L'Insaisissable Protée.* Paris: Belles Lettres, 1953.
Conrad, Joseph. "Novel as World." *Theory of the Novel,* ed. Philip Stevick. New York: Free Press, 1967.
Cordle, Thomas. "Gide and the Novel of the Egoist." *Yale French Studies.* VII, 1951, 91-97.
Delay, Jean. *La Jeunesse d'André Gide.* 2 vols. Paris: Gallimard, 1956-57.
Falk, Eugene H. *Types of Thematic Structure.* Chicago: University of Chicago Press, 1967.
Forster, E. M. *Aspects of the Novel.* New York: Harcourt Brace, 1927.
Fowlie, Wallace. *André Gide, His Life and Art.* New York: Macmillan, 1965.
Friedman, Norman. "Point of View in Fiction: the Development of a Critical Concept." *Theory of the Novel,* ed. Philip Stevick. New York: Free Press, 1967.
Frye, Northrop. *Anatomy of Criticism.* Princeton: Princeton University Press, 1957.
Gide, André. *Dostoevsky.* Translated by Arnold Bennett and Louise Varèse. New York: New Directions, 1961.
———. "Faits-divers." *Nouvelle Revue Française.* XXX (June 1928), 839-849.
———. *Journal 1889-1949.* 2 vols. Bibliothèque de la Pléiade. Paris: Gallimard, 1948-54.
———. *Les Faux-Monnayeurs.* Paris: Gallimard, 1925.
———. *Oeuvres Complètes.* Edition augmentée de textes inédits établie par L. Martin-Chauffier. 15 vols. Paris: Gallimard, 1932-39.
———. *Pretexts; Reflections on Literature and Morality,* ed. Justin O'Brien; translated by Angelo P. Bertocci, Jeffrey J. Carre, Justin O'Brien, and Blanche A. Price. New York: Greenwich Editions, 1959.
Grout, Donald Jay. *A History of Western Music.* New York: W. W. Norton, 1960.
Guerard, Albert J. *André Gide.* New York: E. P. Dutton, 1963.
Hytier, Jean. *André Gide,* translated by Richard Howard. Garden City, N. Y.: Doubleday, 1962.

James, Henry. *The Future of the Novel*. New York: Vintage Books, 1956.
Knight, Everett W. *Literature considered as Philosophy: the French Example*. London: Routledge and Paul, 1957.
La Bruyère, Jean de. "Des Ouvrages de l'Esprit." *Les Caractères ou les Moeurs de ce siècle*. Paris: Garnier Frères, 1962.
Lemaitre, Georges. *Four French Novelists, Marcel Proust, André Gide, Jean Giraudoux, Paul Morand*. London: Oxford University Press, 1938.
Lynes, Carlos. "André Gide and the Problem of Form in the Novel." *Forms of Modern Fiction: Essays Collected in Honor of Joseph Warren Beach*. ed. William Van O'Connor. Minneapolis: University of Minnesota Press, 1948.
Mann, Thomas. "Gide's Unending Search for Harmony." Introduction to Albert J. Guerard, *André Gide*. New York: E. P. Dutton, 1963.
Martin du Gard, Roger. *Oeuvres Complètes*. 2 vols. Paris: Gallimard, 1955.
Ortega y Gasset, José. "Notes on the Novel." *The Dehumanization of Art and Other Essays on Art, Culture, and Literature*. Princeton: Princeton University Press, 1968.
Painter, George D. *André Gide, A Critical Biography*. London: Weidenfeld and Nicolson, 1968.
Priestley, J. B. *Literature and Western Man*. New York: Harper and Row, 1966.
Rossi, Vinio. *André Gide: The Evolution of an Aesthetic*. New Brunswick: Rutgers University Press, 1967.
Sartre, Jean-Paul. "Gide vivant." *Les Temps Modernes*. LXV (March 1951), 1537-41.
Starkie, Enid. "André Gide." *Studies in Modern French Literature*. New Haven: Yale University Press, 1960.
Stevick, Philip, ed. *Theory of the Novel*. New York: Free Press, 1967.
Stock, Irvin. "A View of 'Les Faux-Monnayeurs'." *Yale French Studies*. VII, 1951, 72-80.
Thody, Philip. "'Les Faux-Monnayeurs': The Theme of Responsibility." *Modern Language Review*. LV (July 1960), 351-358.
Valéry, Paul. *Tel Quel* I. Paris: Gallimard, 1941.